Megan,

Keep the faith!

REAL
HOMELAND
SECURITY
The America God Will Bless

REAL HOMELAND SECURITY

The America God Will Bless

RICHARD LAND

BROADMAN
&HOLMAN
PUBLISHERS

NASHVILLE, TENNESSEE

0–8054–2764–3

Published by Broadman & Holman Publishers,
Nashville, Tennessee

Published in association with Alive Communications, Inc.,
7680 Goddard Street, Suite 200, Colorado Springs, Colorado 80920.

Editorial collaboration provided by Helmers Literary Services.

Dewey Decimal Classification: 170
Subject Heading: AMERICAN ETHICS \ AMERICAN—RELIGIOUS
LIFE \ UNITED STATES—MORAL CONDITIONS

Scripture quotations are from the Holy Bible, New International
Version, copyright © 1973, 1978, 1984 by International Bible Society.
Also used is the King James Version.

1 2 3 4 5 6 7 8 9 10 10 09 08 07 06 05 04

If my people, which are called by my name,

shall humble themselves, and

pray, and seek my face, and

turn from their wicked ways,

then will I hear from heaven, and

will forgive their sin,

and will heal their land.

2 CHRONICLES 7:14 KJV

To

Rebekah, my life's partner

for more than thirty years,

without whom nothing would

have been possible!

CONTENTS

PREFACE

As I finished this book and reflected on the two years it took to write, I was reminded of how this project came into being. Not long ago, a reporter asked me: "What does it mean when you say 'God bless America'"? Is that a hope? Is it just an expression? Is it a prayer? Does God bless America because she deserves it? Well, if she deserved it, it wouldn't be a blessing. A blessing is something that is unmerited, something that is above and beyond what we deserve or merit.

Shortly after that conversation with the reporter, I was on a retreat in Colorado Springs with two of my senior staff praying and strategizing about the next five to ten years of our ministry at the ERLC. As we moved through that process, we had finished the first day, and the next morning while I was shaving, God prompted me with one of the things He wanted me to do—it just appeared there on the mirror of my mind and heart. He wanted me to write this book. I put the razor down, wiped the shaving cream off my face, dried my hands, and sat down at the desk in my hotel room where I spent the next few hours in prayer as God gave me the outline for *Real Homeland Security*.

As I kept coming back to that reporter's question, "What does it mean when you say 'God bless America'?" the Lord took me to 2 Chronicles 7:14. The answer was clear. In this passage God defines the conditions for His blessing on any nation—the people of God must get right with Him. So this book you are holding in your hands is the fruit of a two-year project to outline the prayer I am praying for our nation, the promise God has given our nation, and an examination of the divine tipping-point of God's blessing on our nation.

Sometimes we just think God is going to bless America because America is America. But if you just take a moment to stop and look at the America we have become, then ask yourself—Why should God bless America? Is it because we have been killing an unborn baby approximately every twenty seconds for over three decades? Is it because more than half of our children now spend a significant portion of their childhood and adolescence in single parent households? If we stop and think about it, why should God bless America, when we are the world's center for hard-core pornography, when we export pornography through the Internet to every other country in the world and a third of the babies born in the U.S. are born out of wedlock? Has the push to normalize homosexual behavior and sanction same-sex marriage contributed to God's withdrawing His blessings from America?

The bottom line: We can't legislate God's blessing. Remember the account of King Josiah in chapters 22 and 23 of 2 Kings ? The people were totally out of God's will; they weren't even practicing the sacrifices in the temple. Finally they stumbled across the Book of the Law. The king read it, the king's heart was convicted, and he instituted all kinds of positive reforms. Yet his reforms died when he died because only the king's heart was changed. While the people's habits were changed, their hearts were not. The people changed their behavior for a while, but their hearts and their beliefs remained unchanged despite the king's actions. The only way God is going to bless America is for our hearts to change.

I pray that God will use this book to bring revival to your life and to the life of your family and that He will use it to help bring spiritual revival to America. I truly believe that this is the only way that we can have *real* homeland security in the United States of America.

Acknowledgments

I am grateful for the contributions of my many friends and colleagues who shared in the creation of this project. It was truly a team effort, and I am sincerely grateful to all who served in this task, especially Kathy Helmers, who is my writing partner. Her research, reading, gathering of facts, deciphering of my disgraphic scribblings, and phone interviews were invaluable. This project would never have happened without Kathy's help.

I am thankful to my wife, Becky, to whom this book is dedicated. Becky and my three children, Jennifer, Richard, Jr., and Rachel, and my daughter-in-law Chrissie, who are so indescribably special to me! My two proudest titles are husband and dad.

I would also like to express my gratitude to my diligent staff who labor above and beyond the call of duty. God has given me an incredible staff of which I am very appreciative. Thank you—Kerry Bural, Amber Chesser, Pat Clark, Karen Cole, Kim Coleman, Beth Douglas, Barrett Duke, Jacob Fentress, Harold Harper, Dwayne Hastings, Matt Hawkins, Laura Headley, Barbara Jester, Lana Kimbro, Judy Lawson,

Jerry Price, Bobby Reed, Shannon Royce, Tom Strode, Brian Terrell, Sulyn Wilkins, and Dawn Wyatt.

Thanks also to all of my co-laborers and partners in the harvest who listen to our radio programs, *For Faith & Family* and *Richard Land Live!,* who pray for our ministry, and who support us financially. Your prayers and letters of encouragement mean a great deal to our staff and to me personally.

Most of all, I am grateful for my Heavenly Father and God's Son, my Savior, the coming King, Jesus the Christ. May He use this book for His kingdom and His glory and may He continue to bless the United States of America.

I

A PRAYER FOR OUR NATION?

On November 11, 1938, Americans were observing the end of one world war in the shadow of another. It was Armistice Day (now celebrated as Veteran's Day), and 1938 marked exactly two decades after the cease-fire ending World War I. Entertainer Kate Smith was observing the anniversary with a special treat for listeners of her weekly radio program: the debut of a song that would become an unofficial anthem and permanently imprint her voice on a nation's collective memory.

While it seemed as if the lights had gone out on the other side of the ocean as Europe fell under the darkest totalitarianism the world had yet seen in the Third Reich, this song, penned by a Jewish-American composer, sent a beacon of hope and determination through the angry storm clouds of approaching war.

Decades earlier, Irving Berlin had written the song as patriotic entertainment for a military revue. When Kate Smith approached him with her plans for the anniversary broadcast, however, he thoroughly revised the lyrics with serious, prayerful intent. Through the power of radio, "God Bless America" became an instant success.

The then relatively new medium, radio remains a wonderful vehicle for reaching vast numbers of people across the nation who would never darken a church doorway. I am convinced that if the apostle Paul were alive today, he'd be on radio. Now Peter, with his personal charisma and magnetic personality, would be on television, but Paul would be using radio as a fabulous platform for speaking directly and powerfully into his listeners' ears and hearts.

The times we live in today are no less turbulent than they were in the global conflicts of the early twentieth century. This song has become a virtual national invocation, a musical way of joining hands emotionally around the nation's flagpole. In our post–9-11 world, "God Bless America" has become a benediction on our national suffering from terrorist attacks. It was a prayer when it was first introduced, but is it a prayer now? What does it mean when it crosses the lips of those who don't believe in God, and why do they say it? What does it mean when Christians say it? *Should* God bless America? *Will* God bless America? And what would that America look like?

These are not idle questions, because what God does or doesn't do in our country is no idle matter. I hope that by the time you finish reading this book, you will realize what a critical role you can play in our nation's history. If each of us asks these questions with the sincere intent of seeking God's answers, there is no telling what marvels God might choose to do through us. If we ignore them, we do so at our personal and national peril.

SPIRITUAL STATE OF THE UNION

Let's start with a reality check on the spiritual state of America. If America perishes, she will die from self-inflicted wounds. This is not a popular message, especially in an age that values personal choice above all else.

> If America perishes, she will die from self-inflicted wounds. ⟶

There was a prophet in Israel's history who preached the same message to an indifferent and often hostile crowd. Jeremiah warned that the nation's captivity by the Babylonians was God's way of calling the people to repent and seek Him. But his countrymen were convinced that the only way to overcome their conquerors was through a strategic alliance with their former oppressor, Egypt. Jeremiah called Israel to dependence on God alone. It was not a popular message.

In Jeremiah 6:17 God describes His prophets as watchmen: "I appointed watchmen over you and said, 'Listen to the sound of the trumpet!' But you said, 'We will not listen.'" This metaphor would have conjured up extremely familiar images to Jeremiah's audience. Back then, if you lived in a village or a town of any size, there would have been a wall around it. That was the only earthly way a community could protect itself from outside attack. It was your only temporal hope for securing home, family, and neighborhood. The wall had gates permitting people to go in and out, but they were always manned by watchmen. These guards had assigned watches and assigned places along the wall, so that at any time during day or night there was constant surveillance on the entire circumference of the horizon. At the first hint of possible trouble, these watchmen would blow a warning blast on their shofars—long, loud trumpets to rouse people from sleep at night or call them from workday tasks to man their preassigned places on the wall and repel any threat.

As the townspeople would go about their business, they could look up at the wall from any point in the city and see the familiar, comforting presence of the watchmen. When God sent His prophets to the people, He made sure the prophets scanned the horizon carefully. But He also directed their gaze inward, to look for threats to the people's well-being from within their own walls. The Book of Jeremiah is a virtual blast from the prophet's shofar trumpet that the worst dangers lay within.

That is just the situation we are in today, at the dawn of a new century. We face a far greater peril from our own immorality and degradation and degeneracy than we ever faced from the Japanese

Navy or the German Air Force or the Soviet Missile Command. Americans as a whole have more wealth than ever before in our history. Yet, the ironic reality is that Americans have never been more pessimistic and unhappy about their personal present and their personal future. I believe this is because we've been trying to feed our spiritual needs with material food and we're suffering from spiritual and emotional malnutrition.

The verses in Jeremiah 6 immediately preceding reference to the watchmen describe our state of the union: "From the least to the greatest, all are greedy for gain; prophets and priests alike, all practice deceit" (Jeremiah 6:13). We have made idols of our material well-being, and they have come back to haunt us. Lies are rampant at all levels. One former president practiced and rehearsed his lies to the American people. Some think he should be proud of making the latest edition of *Bartlett's Quotations* with, "Let me tell you one thing and I want you to listen to me, I never had sexual relations with that woman, Miss Lewinsky," and "It depends on what the meaning of *is* is." While the president was rehearsing these lies for his statements to the American people, a leader of the opposing party, former House Speaker Newt Gingrich, was carrying on an adulterous affair, proving unfaithful to his second wife and lying about it. Republicans, Democrats and Independents, North and South, East and West, city folk and country folk, all are far too practiced in deceit.

"Are they ashamed of their loathsome conduct?" the prophet asks. It used to be that when people did shameful things, at least they were embarrassed. "No, they have no shame at all; they do not even know how to blush" (Jeremiah 6:15). Now they hire an agent, go on the electronic equivalent of the old-time carnival freak show called day-time talk television, and parade their degradation and degeneracy for the titillation of the audience. And it says more about us than it does about them because if we didn't watch they wouldn't be on television. We have become a nation of electronic "Peeping Toms."

No Shame

Jeremiah 6:16 records how the people refused God's offer of sanctuary from their sin and shame: "This is what the LORD says: 'Stand at the crossroads and look; ask for the ancient paths, ask where the good way is, and walk in it, and you will find rest for your souls. But you said, "We will not walk in it."'"

A few weeks before the presidential election in November 2000, a reporter from one of the major New York papers called me. "Dr. Land, I want to ask you a question," he said. "Is God a Republican?"

"Absolutely not," I replied. "And that is a blasphemous question. It's offensive and insulting because you cannot reduce God to any mere human formulation, least of all a political party. But I will tell you that God is pro-life."

There's a compelling reason why among all the ancient civilizations of the Mediterranean Basin, the Jews alone refrained from practicing abortion and infanticide. The Greeks did it, the Romans did it, the Hittites did it, the Assyrians did it, and the Egyptians did it. But the Israelites didn't, because their God had told them He was involved when conception took place. In the midst of his penitence over his sin, King David declared by divine inspiration that he had a sin nature at his conception (Psalm 51:5). Only a human being, with a soul and a spirit, can have a sin nature.

Psalm 139 describes how God knitted them together in their mother's womb, and all of their parts were written in His book before any of them came to be. Jeremiah's call from God affirms, "Before I formed you in the womb I knew you; before you were born I set you apart; I appointed you as a prophet to the nations" (Jeremiah 1:5).

Many generations back, long before Jeremiah's parents or grandparents were born, God was working to bring about the unique genetic combination that was Jeremiah. And He has done the same with the never-to-be-duplicated genetic combination that is you. If you have siblings, ask yourself if you are different from your brother and sister. (Aren't you grateful?) Yet you had the same mom and the same dad.

We're all unique, every one of us. God created each of us for a unique purpose in His plan for our lives, and it's tailor-made for us, not for anybody else. No one else but you can do as good a job at being the person God created you to be. And God never created a nobody. Everybody is a somebody to God.

I'm grateful to my denomination for encouraging us—and I mean *really* encouraging us—to memorize Scripture when we were children and retain those passages more easily. Whoever picked the particular verses sure knew what they were doing, because Ephesians 2:8–10 has worked its way into my heart and life: "For by grace are ye saved through faith; and that not of yourselves: it is the gift of God: Not of works, lest any man should boast. For we are his workmanship, created in Christ Jesus unto good works, which God hath before ordained that we should walk in them" (KJV). In other words, "before ordained" means there are literal footprints out there, the unique pathway God has ordained for each one of us to walk in following Christ's will for our particular lives.

God has a plan, and He has a purpose for every one of us, including the more than 40 million American babies that have been killed since 1973. I remember sitting in high school, studying the Civil War, and wondering how on earth people could have thought it was all right to own other people. How could they presume it was morally acceptable to turn someone else into property?

Little could I have imagined, sitting there in the 1960s, that in my own lifetime people would presume to say that unborn babies with beating hearts and measurable brain waves are not people but property, and could therefore be destroyed and sold off in body parts . . .

or conceived in order to be harvested as tissue for medical treatments to sustain other human beings.

When we allow human beings to be conceived and then killed to harvest their tissue at ten days of gestation for embryonic stem cell research, we have become biotech cannibals, devouring our young for our own benefit, and bringing upon ourselves the judgment of God. I can remember as a twelve-year-old boy saying to my father and mother at the dinner table, "Today in Sunday school we read about how God's chosen people, the Israelites, had become so sinful that they were taking their little infant babies down into the Valley of Gehenna and offering them up in child sacrifice to the pagan god Moloch." Then I turned to my father and asked, "Daddy, how could they do that?"

My father replied, "I don't know, boy. That's awful, isn't it?"

It was simply unimaginable to those of us sitting around that dining room in Houston, Texas, in the late 1950s that we would live to see an America where there is a baby being killed by abortion every twenty seconds, three babies a minute, one hundred eighty babies an hour, four thousand babies a day, every day. We have killed one out of every three babies conceived in America since 1973—*a 33 percent fatality rate.* We didn't have a 33 percent fatality rate at Omaha Beach. We didn't have a 33 percent fatality rate at Iwo Jima.

The Bible tells us that children are an inheritance from God, yet the most dangerous place for an American citizen is in his or her mother's womb, between conception and birth. America is like the prodigal son: we've taken the inheritance of our unborn children, gone to a far city, and wasted that inheritance in riotous living. Now we're reduced to feeding among the swine for the husks of life.

Have we aborted the next Billy Graham? He could be thirty-one years old if he hadn't been killed in his mother's womb in 1973. Have we aborted the next Abe Lincoln? He could be thirty and fresh out of law school if he hadn't been aborted in 1974. Have we aborted the girl God was knitting and embroidering together in her mother's womb to become a research scientist and find the cure for cancer? She could be twenty-nine and graduated from medical school if she hadn't been aborted in 1975. There's a one-in-three chance that that is precisely what we have done.

Have we aborted the next Billy Graham?

We have denigrated and devalued life. We have practiced child sacrifice because at least one parent considers that baby to be too embarrassing, too expensive, too ill, or too inconvenient. Yet we tolerate all this nonsense of "I'm personally opposed to abortion, but who am I to try to impose my morality on someone else?" Did you know that this very same argument was used by supporters of slavery? I did my senior thesis at Princeton on the slavery controversy. I can point to editorials that announce personal opposition to slavery coupled with reluctance to impose personal morality on slave owners. Of course, the problem with that argument is that no one is protesting how the slave owners imposed their personal immorality on the slaves by holding them in involuntary servitude. And when people kill an unborn baby they're imposing their immorality on an unborn child. It's always a fatal imposition, because the baby dies. We have a responsibility— a moral obligation—to say, "You will do that no more." Until we do, God will continue to judge us as a nation for this sin.

WE ARE ALL INVOLVED

But it isn't just those active in immorality who are helping to drag America down to unprecedented lows. We are blessed to live in a democracy, and despite the views of Christians who say we shouldn't seek to change our nation's morality through the political process, the reality is that the spiritual state of our union is powerfully influenced by how we vote, and whether we participate in the public policy process or not.

I was sensitized to political issues in childhood because I grew up in a bicultural home. My dad is from Texas, and my mother is from Boston. It's a really interesting combination. They canceled out each other's vote in virtually every election. My dad is what they call in

Texas a "Yellow Dog Democrat." My mother is what they call in Massachusetts a "Rock-ribbed Republican," which is a New England version of a Yellow Dog Democrat. I'm not telling you anything I haven't told my parents, but they were both wrong when my dad was voting for Adlai Stevenson and my mother was voting for Dwight Eisenhower; when my dad was voting for John F. Kennedy and my mother was voting for Richard Nixon; when my dad was voting for Lyndon B. Johnson and my mother was voting for Barry Goldwater. They were both wrong because they were voting the traditions and the loyalties of their families and region of the country instead of voting their shared core values, beliefs, and convictions.

Our loyalty does not belong to any political party, and it doesn't belong to any candidate. It belongs to God Almighty. And God cares about how we vote. Let me make this crystal clear. If Dr. Laura, an observant Jew, is running for president on the pro-life ticket, saving babies but promising to raise taxes 50 percent, and her opponent is a Southern Baptist from Tennessee who says he's going to protect a woman's right to choose, but will slash taxes 50 percent, I'm going to vote for life and against my pocketbook every time. Why? I don't want to have to explain to God someday why I did otherwise.

When God commissioned Jeremiah, the prophet protested that youth and inexperience rendered him unfit for the task. But God assured Jeremiah of His presence and protection, indeed of the very words Jeremiah would speak: "Then the LORD reached out his hand

and touched my mouth and said to me, 'Now, I have put my words in your mouth'" (Jeremiah 1:9). The prophet's words were first spoken to God's people Judah as they stood with their toes curled over the edge of the precipice of the coming judgment from Babylon, because they refused to repent and obey God. Let's not forget that if God would judge His chosen people by sending them into captivity in Babylon, He won't refrain from judging us. But neither will God leave us without His counsel, to bring us back to Him and restore us to His blessing instead of His judgment.

GOD'S CONDITIONS OF BLESSING

Clearly, for evangelical Christians, "God Bless America" is a fervent prayer, not simply a national slogan. We take God seriously, and we take God's blessing seriously. But America is not a single entity or people group; it is a living, breathing nation made up of millions of families and hundreds of thousands of communities. How on earth can we discern what God's conditions would be for blessing America?

God has already established the conditions under which He will bless America, and what that America would look like. This primary Scripture passage provides a blueprint for restoration of a nation. It offers a prescription for any person, couple, family, community, or church that finds itself far from God:

If my people, which are called by my name, shall humble themselves, and pray, and seek my face, and turn from their wicked ways; then will I hear from heaven, and will forgive their sin, and will heal their land. (2 Chronicles 7:14 KJV)

However, we can't apply this passage without understanding the context of this promise and how it applies today. Who *are* God's people today? What are the conditions under which God will bless our country? And what will it look like? Who is the man God will bless, the woman God will bless, the husband and wife God will bless? Who is the family God will bless? What is the church God will bless? What is the community God will bless? And what kind of government will God bless?

---

*O*ur loyalty does not belong to any political party, and it doesn't belong to any candidate. It belongs to God Almighty. ⌒

I'll never forget a time when our family was driving down a long, long highway. Our children's ages were five years, two years, and eleven months. (Need I say more?) Like all parents, my wife and I were doing just about everything we could possibly think of to do to maintain sanity in the car. We were singing every song we knew, and we got to the refrain, "The king is coming, the king is coming. Praise God, the king is coming."

My five-year-old interrupted to ask, "Daddy, what's a king?" I must confess that I never did successfully answer any of my three children's questions until they reached age twelve without an interpretation and a translation from my wife. So I replied by prompting my wife, "Honey, tell Jennifer what a king is."

My wife said, "Well, Jennifer, a king is somebody who tells you what to do."

And my sweet little princess Jennifer Rebekah, precious innocent five-year-old, said without batting an eye, "Well, I don't want anybody to tell *me* what to do."

There it is, I thought. *There's the sin nature, right there.* "I don't want anybody to tell me what to do." I want to do what *I* want to do, when *I* want to do it.

God hasn't changed. We must remember what it is like when we are right with Him, and recognize when it's not that way anymore—and then return to where we lost it and repent.

To pray "God bless America" while living as if we are under no one's authority but our own is to ensure that we will never taste the promised blessing. But to pray it while turning back to God, repenting, and seeking Him, ensures that we will taste nothing less than His faithfulness in restoring us to live out His plans for His purposes.

2

A Promise for Our Nation?

What's wrong with America? I'll give you the good, the bad, and the ugly. The good is that, according to George Barna's research,[1] 40 percent of Americans know enough about what it means to be a born-again Christian to claim to be one, acknowledging that they trust Jesus alone for their salvation. The bad is that 40 percent of Americans believe Jesus was just a man, and He sinned while He was on earth. The ugly is that only 14 percent of Americans say they try to live their lives according to the ethical and moral standards of the Bible. That means that almost twice as many people who claim to be Christians don't even try to base their behavior and goals on the Bible's teaching.

If the American people would humble themselves *en masse* and meet the conditions of God's promise in 2 Chronicles 7:14, could we expect that as a consequence, God would bless America?

Let's take a closer look at this passage and its biblical background. The immediate context for this promise is the culmination of one of the glories of the ancient world: Solomon's temple, designed and built according to God's detailed specifications. The Ark of the Covenant could now reside in the most holy of holy places. When Solomon finished his prayer of dedication, fire came down from heaven to consume the sacrifices, and God's *shekinah* glory filled the temple. The people responded with worship and awe. This encounter of a holy God dwelling with His fallen but redeemed people depicted the grace of God's love, in which He bound Himself irrevocably and unilaterally in a covenant He chose to make with His people.

> *Instead* of praying for our nation's repentance, we might do better to pray for contrite hearts, for revival among individuals that will lead to personal and social change.

This time was a kind of apex of God's blessing of His people. Clearly, they were fulfilling the conditions of 2 Chronicles 7:14 during this period. After a seven-day festival to celebrate the completion of this magnificent structure, God appeared to Solomon. First He affirmed that He had heard Solomon's prayer of dedication, and that He had chosen the temple as a place of holy sacrifice and atonement. But He also knew that with fallen human beings, there would come a time when they would stray once again. So He issued a warning that if the people again strayed from obedience to Him, He would seek to restore them through various means of judgment: drought, insect plagues, disease. Yet He would not abandon them to their own unfaithfulness, leaving them in judgment. He would also pour out blessing upon them the moment they returned to Him in humility, prayer, seeking Him, and forsaking unrighteousness. The people could count on God's healing forgiveness and acceptance.

How do we make applications from how God worked with the Israelites in their day to how He works with us in our day? The Old Testament provides a relatively clear picture of God's dealing with His chosen people. Today, God's people are dispersed as the body of Christ across many nations.

Instead of praying for our nation's repentance, we might do better to pray for contrite hearts, for revival among individuals that will lead to personal and social change. Some call for the country to repent for having supported slavery and enforced segregation. But repentance is individual. I can't repent for what my great-grandfather did. I can apologize, express remorse, and ask for forgiveness, but I can repent only for what *I* do. If my great-grandfather owned slaves, my repentance doesn't do him any good. He has to deal with God for his sins; I can't do that for him.

But if enough individuals repent, they can become a trigger for God's blessing. We have no way of knowing what critical mass of individuals, all of whom are Christians and living Christianly, might prove to be the divine tipping point for God's blessing. But I do believe that when enough Christians in our country fulfill God's conditions enumerated in 2 Chronicles 7:14, God will send revival and pour out His blessings on America once again. That is a promise we can stand on.

DOES JUDGMENT ALWAYS PRECEDE BLESSING?

The spiritual state of our union has many parallels with the spiritual condition of Israel in Jeremiah's time. Priests and prophets were denounced for their immorality and deceit (see Jeremiah 5:30–31), and the people were denounced for loving to have it that way.

Do you know why there was such rapid decay in America in the last half century? Because there was *a failure of faith* and *a failure of nerve* in the pulpit—primarily in the mainline denominations, but no denomination escaped untainted. We had the dry-rot in ours, I can tell you. Only one thing to do with dry-rot: cut it out. Preachers who preach falsely say that God is a God of love, and so He loves you just the way you are. That's half true. He does love you the way you are, but that doesn't mean He doesn't want you to change.

Years ago when our children were small and my parents were visiting us, our daughter chose the opportunity to express her creativity with crayon on the invitingly pristine walls of our hallway. She denied responsibility for the graffiti, but I knew very well that she'd done it—if you're a parent, you know that most of the time, discerning your children's guilt or lack thereof isn't rocket science. So I took her in the bathroom along with a ruler, gave her three swats, and came out with her.

Do you know why there was such rapid decay in America in the last half century? Because there was *a failure of faith* and *a failure of nerve* in the pulpit.

My mother was standing in the hall just outside the bathroom—in *tears*. Now mind you, this is the same woman who broke a hairbrush on me in my youth.

I said, "Where's dad?"

She sniffed and said, "He went out to the back yard." *Rather than subject himself to this treatment of his granddaughter,* was her implication.

In my childhood, my father once discovered me out in the hallway outside Training Union, which my brother and I attended every Sunday night. As he came walking by he asked, "Son, what are you doing out here?"

"Well, Daddy," I replied, "they threw me out." Now, in my own defense I want to explain that had I been paying enough attention to know they were praying, I would have waited until they finished the prayer before I popped the balloon.

He responded by giving me a spanking right then and there.

Then he thought about it all during church. When we got home he spanked me again.

But I tell you, the way my parents reacted to my daughter's behavior, you'd think they would have cut her drawings straight out of the sheetrock and taken them down to the frame shop to exclaim, "Look what our little granddaughter did!"

God is a father, not a grandfather. Those of you who have been close to your grandfathers know the difference. Fathers spank; grandfathers spoil. It was a great revelation to me to watch my parents become grandparents. If they had raised me that way, I'd be in the penitentiary!

The great lie perpetrated by the devil is that God is a grandfather. The Bible doesn't say anything about God the Grandfather. It says a lot about God the Father, who chastises those who are His children. Jeremiah chapter 5 punctuates its description of the Israelites' unrighteousness with the Father's reproach, "Should I not punish them for this?' declares the LORD. 'Should I not avenge myself on such a nation as this?'" (v. 9, 29).

Clearly, there are consequences to sin. And they are not just spiritual consequences. Was it happenstance that an earthquake's epicenter in California was about two miles from where 90 percent of the pornography is produced in the United States? I don't think so.

Now we have to be careful when disasters occur, because they don't always signify God's judgment. We live in a world that is racked by the results of the curse of sin. Does that mean that God never uses supposedly natural catastrophes to judge His people? The Bible indicates otherwise.

God makes it clear that if His people stray from Him, He will bring judgment upon them. Does that mean that He judges the sin of His people more harshly than He does the sins of others? That seems to be the strong implication in the New Testament. He doesn't judge those who are not true Christians because they are going to spend eternity paying for their sins. That is judgment enough, and it will be rendered in the next life. But as Christians, our sins have already been paid for by Jesus. And we sin against greater light than non-Christians do. So the heavenly Father is far more likely to chastise us in the here and now.

God's word to Solomon in 2 Chronicles 7:14 indicates that judgment precedes blessing. God uses judgment to get our attention so that He can bless us when we turn back to Him. This is the work of a Father in our lives. Personally, I have never been aware of a situation in which a person was being judged by God for continued rebellious sin in their lives, and they didn't realize it. If you have to wonder whether a disaster is a judgment from God, and you are seeking God honestly, then it probably isn't judgment. Most of us have either experienced, or know others who experienced, the hand of God upon us to get our attention when we weren't listening.

God is a father, not a grandfather.

Some Christians who persist in unrepentant sin may not recognize God's judgment until they are ushered into eternity. I knew of a very prominent Christian leader in the 1960s who was considered one of our finest preachers. He was tall, good-looking, and endowed with a personal charisma that attracted others to him—especially women. He fanned that flame, and he fell into illicit affairs with several different women. One day while he was on a road trip, he was overcome by fatigue and pulled off on the side of the road to rest. An eighteen-wheeler veered off the road and killed him. Did God take his life because he refused to repent? Quite possibly.

Another man I knew was a very successful pastor of one of the largest churches in the world. His involvement in multiple extra-marital affairs with women in the church cost him his ministry and eventually his wife, who forgave him the first time but called it quits when he kept doing it after she took him back.

A few years later, he had an operation to remove a brain tumor. While he was being prepped, a friend of his who was still in the ministry kept him company and prayed with him. He began to weep, saying, "I'm so sorry. I know I let the Lord down. I let you all down. I let my family down. I let everyone down. I'm so sorry." They wheeled him into surgery, and he died. I don't think his close friends had any question personally that he died prematurely because of his sin. Those in ministry are much more likely to find their lives shortened by unconfessed sin because they can do so much more damage than others through their hypocrisy. When I see men who are enmeshed in such chronic sins and nothing happens to them, I must assume they are unsaved and illegitimate, because the Father does not chastise them as sons.

CHANGE SOCIETY OR WIN SOULS?

There's a wonderful book by Charles Ryrie, entitled *Balance in the Christian Life,* in which he points out that virtually every doctrinal error perpetrated on the body of Christ results from a loss of balance in understanding or practice. One aspect of the Christian life is emphasized to the exclusion of something else, whereas the Scripture is divinely balanced. The Bible makes very clear that our primary relationship is vertical, between God and each of us through Jesus Christ. But we have a second important relationship that is horizontal: with our fellow human beings. You can visualize the cross as a symbol for remembering these two in priority order. The vertical pole is greater than, and supports, the horizontal beam. But without the horizontal beam, there is no cross—no intersection of God and humanity, no permeation of the Gospel into all of human life.

The Lord has clearly established our obligations not simply to other believers but also to our neighbors, to those who disagree with us and even oppose us, to those who cannot protect themselves. We are called to be salt and light, bringing the good news of the Gospel and living out the good works of the Gospel, evangelizing individuals and becoming a force for righteousness in society. In my own faith tradition, which is shared by many evangelicals, we have always understood this dual responsibility. Christians must "seek to make the will of Christ supreme in our own lives and in human society. . . . Every Christian should seek to bring industry, government, and society as a whole under the sway of the principles of righteousness, truth, and brotherly love."[2]

Bringing the Gospel to bear on the social order is a biblical mandate. But it is also a corrective for times when personal righteousness lives side by side with, and even supports, unrighteousness and injustice. A classic example is segregation: the most churched part of society, the South, had many fine Christian people who either were blind to the racism or felt it was not the church's responsibility to alleviate injustice.

If you go back to the slavery era, you can find some of the most vocal supporters of slavery within the church—and some of the most vocal critics of slavery, as well. The problem is that although personal righteousness is important, we still have to have some way to deal with the injustice that is done by that percentage of the population that is not redeemed, and is not going to be redeemed. They will continue to exploit, to rape, to rob, and to cause suffering among people who are unable to protect themselves. That's why God ordained civil government: to punish those who do evil and reward those who do right. The redeemed have an obligation not only to evangelize, but also to protect the unredeemed from the unredeemed.

CAN GOD EVER BLESS AMERICA?

Some raise the question of whether God will *ever* be able to bless America without compromising His character, because only when all of America becomes Christian can God bless it accordingly. This view purports that it is a waste of time for Christians to work for godly change in our social structures, because authentic change takes place only in people's hearts. Therefore we should focus all our efforts on evangelism, because the kingdom can be ushered in only in individual hearts, one at a time. For example:

When the church invests time, money, and human
energy in political causes, we waste our resources. . . .
Our energies should not be spent just trying to make
sinners better people. . . . The will of the Lord [in
Ephesians 5:16–17] is clear: we are called to preach the
message of reconciliation and implore people to be rec-
onciled to God. To do something else is to be foolish
and to waste time and resources. We're not interested
in making cosmetic changes to our nation's moral
climate.[3]

Few evangelicals would argue that all of society is going to be
redeemed through our evangelistic efforts. Therefore, we must seek to
protect people from exploitation by others so that even the unredeemed will behave far better toward their neighbors than they would
otherwise. We need to extend societal protection to racial and ethnic
minorities, so that no one is denied his basic constitutional rights
because of the color of his skin. We cannot allow women to be denied
their basic constitutional rights because they are female. We cannot
allow people to be denied their basic constitutional rights because
they're not born yet.

Yes, we should seek to win people to Jesus and to teach people who
have come to know Jesus as Savior that every baby is precious and
should never be aborted. But we also have an obligation to defend
those babies conceived by mothers who are not saved. We are morally

obligated to ensure that people are not allowed to kill their sick and elderly relatives. If we didn't have laws against slavery, some people would still own slaves. They wouldn't give a rip that you and I thought they were horrible. If we didn't have laws against segregation, we'd have even more racism than exists now.

I am *not* saying that focusing on evangelism is wrong. It is indeed the right focus. But it is not the *only* legitimate focus for Christians in secular society. When it is affirmed over against social change, it can foster a circle-the-wagons orientation. Christians can't be of much good in society if they are hiding from it. They also cannot fulfill Christ's mandate to be salt and light in society if they withdraw from it.

The evangelism-only position goes too far when it condemns "moralism," the practice of doing right and not doing wrong, as a dangerous distraction from the true work of the church: "There are occasionally some temporal, superficial benefits to be gained by using the democratic process to mitigate public indecency and to oppose immoral policies."[4] Although it is true that God will never bless America because of moralism alone, that does not mean we should quit trying to bring reform to the social sphere. The abolition of slavery was no superficial benefit. The Civil Rights Movement was not a tepid improvement in our moral temperature: it was a decisive force in eliminating injustice and helping to bring both society and church under the sway of righteousness.

Of course, if social improvement is devoid of genuine evangelical revival, there will be no blessing by God. That doesn't mean that we should put all of our efforts into conversion and none into social reform. Conversely, pietistic individual devotion without opposition to social injustice will not be blessed by God. That doesn't mean that we should abandon missions and invest all resources in governmental reform and social ministries. The biblical mandates for righteous living based on the saving grace of God in Jesus Christ do not allow us to split these dimensions into "either-or" options. If you have one without the other, you have a flawed option—or, as Charles Ryrie would observe, a biblical imbalance.

Warnings about the "deadly danger of moralism" can have the effect of pulling Christians out of the public sphere by dismissing the good because it is not the best:

> What can Christians do to help halt the spiritual
> and moral decline in America? Many believe the best
> solutions are political activism, judicial challenges,
> public protests, organized boycotts, educational pro-
> grams, and other kinds of organized civic efforts. By
> such means they hope to elevate the standard of moral-
> ity in American society and thereby win God's blessing
> for our nation.
>
> On a purely human level, the rationale behind that
> kind of thinking is easy to understand. The court,

legislature, and even local school boards have partici-
pated in systematically undermining the morality of
America. . . . It is right for us to oppose the sins of our
society, and it is right that Christians as individuals
should voice their objection in the voting booth and
by speaking out in other ways. But are political movements and moral crusades the ultimate answers to the
evils that threaten America? Can spiritual decline in
our nation be reversed through legislation and moral
reform alone?[5]

Well, of course the answer is no: spiritual decline cannot be reversed
through moral reform alone. But it is wrong to condemn any organ-
ized activity by Christians and dilute the potential of their influence
through social vehicles such as the voting booth and speaking out in
public. These activities are not a waste of time. It is never a waste of
resources to be obedient to Christ.

God has called us to the Great Commission, and God has called
us to serve others. He never called us to do just one or the other. Our
purpose is to shine as light and to season as salt. God is also not going
to bless us if we Christians know to do good and don't do it. Being
salt means stopping the decay of the unconverted who continue to
prey on underage children in child pornography, to kill unborn
babies, to engage in acts of hatred against other people. Of course, we
are to seek to convert people, and let God bring them into right

relationship with Him. When Christians get right with God, they are impelled to go out into the world seeking to bring morality where there is immorality.

BALANCING PERSONAL AND SOCIAL RIGHTEOUSNESS

Christ has called us to personal righteousness, and He has called us to societal righteousness. To separate one from the other is to violate both and to pursue a truncated and incomplete discipleship.

The Civil Rights Movement is a prime example of why social action is a legitimate focus in seeking God's blessing upon America. Is racism contrary to the Gospel? Yes. Is bigotry contrary to the Gospel? Yes. Is denying people their rights contrary to the Gospel? Yes. And Christians were too often the ones helping to perpetrate it! Martin Luther King, Jr. forced Christians to confront the disconnect between what their faith taught and how they were behaving. Eventually, that caused a change in behavior.

But some Christians will go so far in asserting personal righteousness over against social righteousness that they will dismiss as irrelevant the work of a leader such as Dr. King because his personal righteousness was corrupted through persistent moral failure. We need to view Martin Luther King, Jr. honestly, warts and all. We can acknowledge his failures with sadness and grief, but we don't have to condemn the man and his ministry.

When I teach courses in seminaries, I often assign my students a book called *The Southern Front,* by Eugene Genovese, a former professor of mine. When I studied under Dr. Genovese, he was a Marxist. But in his book, Genovese wrote a chapter on a slave owner who was overcome with remorse after the war and, realizing that he had not been a good husband to his first wife, committed himself to trying harder to be a much better husband to his second wife. It was clear to me that this author was on a spiritual journey. I commented to my wife, "I think either Genovese is a Christian, or he will soon become one." Less than two years later, it was announced that he had returned to the faith of his youth—Catholicism—and it was soon evident that he had truly become a Christian.

The Southern Front devotes a long chapter to Dr. King. My students in their twenties and thirties had never read anything like it because it they were unlikely to find a sympathetic view of Dr. King in the circles they traveled in. Genovese has much the same perspective on Dr. King that I have: a great deal of admiration for Dr. King, enormous respect for what he accomplished, awe at the incredible courage it took to do what he did, and sadness over his personal moral failures. The reality is, it's amazing he lived as long as he did, because it was virtually a foregone conclusion that he would be killed by the fierce and evil opposition he faced.

At the same time, Genovese deals honestly and forthrightly with Dr. King's moral failures.

Dr. King was a great man with severe flaws: rampant plagiarism in his doctoral dissertation; chronic sexual immorality in the form of serial adultery; and heavy drinking, most likely a consequence of his unrelieved guilt. Some evangelicals are particularly harsh in judging him because they rightly hold ministers to a higher standard than politicians. Others simply don't like being reminded how wrong they were in opposing the Civil Rights Movement.

There is evidence that in the final year and a half of his life, King was returning to the simple biblical literalism of his father, who had a fundamentalist faith. The son was reclaiming his biblical roots because he could find nothing in the liberal Protestant theology of the mid-twentieth century to explain the palpable evil that he faced everyday. If human beings were basically good, then he wouldn't have been dealing with such fierce opposition from people who were so consumed by racial prejudice they were willing to shoot down Medgar Evers in front of his home and blow up little girls in a church in Birmingham.

I have little question that Dr. King had a conversion experience when he was a child or a teenager. He was wracked with guilt over his sexual immorality. There is a big difference between being sorry for your failure to live up to what you know is right, and being sorry you got caught. It's clear Dr. King was having real difficulty dealing with his own failure to live up to what he knew was right.

"The only thing necessary for evil to triumph is for good men to do nothing," wrote Edmond Burke to a colleague in 1795. The redeemed have a personal obligation to behave in ways that are pleasing to God. But we also have an obligation to seek to have society reflect God's standards of right and wrong. Our desire for God's blessing should not be for our welfare alone, but for the welfare of all those whom God loves.

I remember clearly the first time I ever heard the song "God Bless America." I was a young boy, not yet a teenager, and I was attending a patriotic observance. I heard many songs at that event—"America the Beautiful," "The Battle Hymn of the Republic," "The Star-Spangled Banner," among others—but this one had a strangely powerful effect on me, stirring me as did none of the others. Since then, throughout my life, hearing the song performed has never failed to move me. The lyrics and melody blend in a wonderful unity.

Perhaps you find this song deeply moving as well. Together, let's ask God to turn this response into a deep and powerful longing for God's blessing. Let's pray that this longing would sweep into the hearts of His people across our nation.

3

WHO ARE GOD'S PEOPLE TODAY?

A reporter from the *Los Angeles Times* once called me to ask about who God's people are. "Arabs say they are part of the seed of Abraham," she suggested; "doesn't that mean that they get the promise and blessing, too?"

I replied, "You know, Abraham tried that. In Genesis 17, we learn that he asked God, 'Let my son Ishmael find favor in your sight.' And God said, 'I have heard your prayer, Abraham, and I will make of Ishmael a great nation.' Last time I checked," I continued, "there were over three hundred million Arabs in the world. They are descended from Ishmael. But the promise is given through the seed of promise, Isaac. God promised the land of Canaan to the seed of Abraham and Isaac forever. He promised to bless those who bless the Jews and curse those who curse the Jews."

I went on to describe how the century we have just lived through gave us perhaps the most dramatic proof of this promise we have ever seen. Germany tried to kill all the Jews in an insane genocidal crusade. The result: Germany flattened, conquered, and nine million Germans killed in World War II. Over a hundred thousand German women and girls were raped by the Russian Army as they stormed into East Germany. The nation was split apart right down the middle, and half of it remained in brutal occupation for the next fifty years.

Russia, as anti-Semitic as Germany—just not as efficient at it— lost 20 million of its people to World War II. And the Russian government killed 35-40 million more of its own people.

Compare the modern history of Russia and Germany with that of the United States. We have been the least anti-Semitic country in the world, and God has blessed this country despite her sin and idolatry. Why? When a nation blesses God's chosen people, God blesses that nation.

We need to bless the Jews more than the Jews need us to bless them, because they have an ally far stronger than all our national strength and resources and wisdom combined. Their ally is called the Lion of Judah, and He always keeps His promises.

God and Country

"God and country" are often tossed together to signal a certain kind of patriotism, sometimes with a few other elements for local color: mom, guns, apple pie. It usually means that "God is on our side," and therefore, by very loose reasoning, the presumption is sometimes extended to include, "and we are God's people."

Our expressions of this phrase may be uniquely American, but this concept is not unique to us. If you lived in Japan, where they engage in worship of their ancestors, as an adherent of Shintoism you might believe that you could perform an act of worship by committing suicide for your country. This practice has become horrifyingly familiar to us from the analogous practice of militant Muslims, who believe they gain eternal benefits by dying for the cause of Palestinian defiance of Israel, killing as many Israelis as possible in the process.

Perhaps the most extreme case of national idolatry or self-worship was Germany under Nazism. Germany abandoned its historic understanding of God many, many years ago. Most of the early twentieth-century theological liberals were Germans. As the German people had their confidence in the God of Scripture taken away, they began to worship themselves and made themselves their own god, presuming they were a master race, with disastrous consequences for themselves and for the whole world.

The "God and country" slogan is problematic not because it is always wrong to link them, but because it is so often based on an inadequate understanding of God, and even more often on an inadequate understanding of the country's weaknesses. Is this country perfect? No. But on the whole—and it is on the whole that we must judge such things—America has been a force for justice and a force for freedom in the world. If all the countries of the world wanted peace and freedom as much as America wants peace and freedom, we would *have* peace and freedom in the world.

Just how Christian is America, anyway?

Patriotic swagger, the "my country—love it or leave it" attitude, often triggers controversy and opposition. Some react against what they perceive as a simplistic adoration of America and a presumption that God is on America's side. Patriotism can become an idol, and its distortions can lead to the kind of extreme and violent behavior that often characterizes survivalists and white supremacists. Others look down on fervent patriotism simply because they hold philosophies and worldviews antithetical to what America has stood for over the centuries. One nation "under God" is an offense to them.

Just how Christian is America, anyway? And should we be praying for a Christian America?

HOW CHRISTIAN IS AMERICA?

The term "Christian America" is sometimes used, erroneously, to describe the philosophical and theological foundations on which our country was built. Has America ever been a Christian nation? No.

Our nation was *founded* on biblical Judeo-Christian principles wedded to enlightenment ideas of self-government. Those ideas work only when a significant segment of the population is voluntarily obeying the law because they are aware of being subject to a higher authority. When this percentage of the population which is voluntarily obeying the law drops below a certain level, then a self-governing democracy doesn't work.

John Adams, our second president and one who labored most diligently to secure our Constitution said in 1798:

> We have no government armed in power capable
> of contending in human passions unbridled by moral-
> ity and religion. Our Constitution was made for a
> moral and religious people. It is wholly inadequate for
> the government of any other.

A genuinely Christian America would mean that every person in America, or at least the vast majority of Americans, has come to a personal faith in Jesus Christ as Lord and Savior—not through government sponsorship or government subsidy, but by the evangelistic action of individual Christians, churches, and mission groups.

If God is not willing that any should perish, but all should come to a full knowledge of the truth (2 Peter 3:9), then when we practice obedience to the Great Commission to go into all the world and preach the Gospel, we would want not just a Christian America, but a Christian world. And the fact that we know that a majority of people are going to reject the Lord does not mean that we shouldn't desire to see every person in America, every person in all the world, come to personal faith in Jesus Christ. Indeed it is our Great Commission responsibility to seek just that.

A genuinely Christian America would mean that every person in America, or at least the vast majority of Americans, has come to a personal faith in Jesus Christ as Lord and Savior. ✐

That does not mean we should focus only on personal conversion. We should also seek to achieve a society that reflects the eternal values revealed in God's Word and which rewards and punishes behavior based on God's understanding of good and evil (Romans 13:1–7).

If God were to bless us according to the conditions of 2 Chronicles 7:14, we would be a far more Christian nation than we are today, because a much larger percentage of our population would be made up of born-again believers who are living their faith. Our efforts are best focused on being God's evangelizing and discipling people—leaving it to God to choose when enough of God's people are meeting the conditions of His promise to unleash His blessing on their land.

This scenario is much different than a theocracy, such as a fundamentalist Muslim regime, where a ruling structure of religious leaders seeks to represent God and institute their understanding of divine law in place of the civil government elected by the people.

Such theocracies claim God's authority for themselves and squelch all dissent. In a representative democracy under the rule of law, like the United States, government should reflect the people's values and beliefs, and should never countenance coercion in matters of conscience and religious faith. An America with an ever-increasing percentage of born-again Christians in the population should increasingly reflect their values, both in laws and social mores.

In the Old Testament, the people of God were generally considered the Israelite nation, but the term particularly signified the *Yahweh-ists,* those who were true believers within that elect nation. In the New Testament context, the people of God are those of the Way, those who trust Jesus Christ as Lord and Savior in all of their manifold expressions from every ethnicity, every tribe, every tongue, every nation.

So, through noncoercive New Testament evangelism, we should set our sights on a nation in which a significant percentage of the population has a personal relationship with Jesus Christ and is trying to humble themselves, pray, seek His face, and turn from their wicked ways.

As each of those people fulfills the conditions of God's promise, he or she will be blessed. Each of their families will be blessed. Churches in which those believers are the dominant membership will be blessed. Communities in which those churches are placed will be blessed. And when some divine critical mass of the population is reached in those communities across the nation, the entire country will be blessed (2 Chronicles 7:14).

MY LAND, YOUR LAND

Christians in America are sometimes criticized for focusing only on themselves and ignoring needs abroad. Slogans such as "God bless Afghanistan" crop up in protest over this perceived ethnocentrism.

One of America's idols is autonomy—absolute individual freedom to do whatever I want to do without someone else telling me it's wrong.

I think that in the providence of God, we are born into a particular country and therefore acquire a sense of national identity. For Americans to pray "God bless America" isn't any different than British citizens praying "God save the queen." If I were a German citizen,

I would probably be praying "God bless Germany." But I'm an American by the providence of God. Part of God's plan for my life, as it is with everybody born in this nation or led to embrace this nation, includes my involved citizenship in this nation.

If God forgives our sin, it is the sin of Christians, not of unbelievers, that He is forgiving. Most unbelievers haven't asked for God's forgiveness, and that forgiveness only comes through personal faith in Jesus Christ as Lord and Savior. However, if Christians bring God's healing upon the land through their repentance and obedience, everyone will experience the promised blessing. We live in America, so it's our land. When the blessings are unleashed, it will be like the rain falling on the just as well as the unjust.

This is true of Christians and unbelievers in any nation. For Americans, "that land" is America; for Canadians, Canada; for Mexicans, Mexico. God will fulfill His promise of blessing in whatever land a sufficient number of Christians invoke it by their belief, repentance, and obedience.

The Bible records how God sent believers first to Jerusalem and then to Judea, Samaria, and the uttermost parts of the world. For Americans, Jerusalem is our local metropolitan area. Judea is our state or region of the country. Since Samaritans were the Jews' detested enemies, Samaria today for us would probably be radical Islamic terrorists, or maybe Saudi Arabia; a decade ago, perhaps Russia. We are not to be myopically limited to the United States in our vision of

God's work in our lives, but for most of us, our existence will be played out in an American context unless God has called us to overseas missions.

It is worthwhile noting that a huge preponderance of the world's missionaries and missions funding are provided by the people of the United States—even though we comprise only 6 percent of the world's population. Do we ignore the world? No. Could we do more? Yes. Most Americans have a sense of their country as playing a critical role in the world as a defender of freedom and religious liberty, and their commitment to their country includes this global mind-set.

GOD'S PEOPLE TODAY

Our sense of America's special role in the world does not mean that we should be drawing parallels between the Israelites and America as a nation especially favored by God. There is only one chosen people— the Jews. This truth was established by the Abrahamic Covenant, in which God made certain promises to the Jews that He did not make to any other people, including Americans.

God established a special covenant relationship with His people Israel. It is unique; the Bible never replicates this relationship. I affirm this as a biblicist and as a Baptist, recognizing that Presbyterian or reformed theology does not agree. Reformed theology erroneously views the New Testament church as the successor to Israel in the Old

Testament, and therefore the promises made to Israel have been transferred to the church as the body of Christ. Circumcision was a sign of the Old Covenant, and so infant baptism is inferred to be a sign of the New Covenant. This is often called "replacement theology" since it asserts that the church has replaced Israel in the plan of God for humanity.

> If God forgives our sin, it is the sin of Christians, not unbelievers, that He is forgiving.

A sizable portion of evangelicals believe, along with most Baptists, that Israel is a type of the church, but is not the church. The church is a New Testament institution. A lot of Reformed Presbyterians believe that the Jews are no longer God's chosen people, because Christians are now the chosen people. This contrasts with the Baptist affirmation that the Bible is very clear that God made certain promises to Israel, and today He is still in the midst of fulfilling those promises to Israel, which are separate and distinct from the New Testament promises to the church as the bride of Christ.

Such Reformed Calvinists mistakenly assume that the church and Israel are the same, so they freely extrapolate from all of the statements about the election of God's people in the Old Testament to the election of individuals in the New Testament. Calvin got his ecclesiology wrong in thinking that the church was Israel, and it skewed his understanding of the doctrine of salvation.

Such Calvinists don't see any distinction between Israel and the church. Those who do see the distinction are much more likely to recognize that there are at least *three* major differences between Old Testament election and New Testament election. *First,* Old Testament election is corporate. God said you (plural) are going to be my people, and I am going to be your God. In the New Testament, God's election is extended to individual believers. *Second,* in the Old Testament, election is to "special people" status, not everyone that was part of the elect nation was saved. In the New Testament, election is to spiritual salvation. And *third,* Old Testament election is not related to, or intertwined with anything. God just said, "You're going to be my people, and I'm going to be your God." In the New Testament, we have two different apostles, Paul and Peter, who say in two separate books that New Testament election is related somehow to the foreknowledge of God. Paul said those He foreknew He did predestinate, (Romans 8:29) and Peter said they were "Elect according to the foreknowledge of the Father . . ." (1 Peter 1:2).

Now it's the argument of people like myself that when you've got such significant differences between New Testament election and Old Testament election, you ought to be extraordinarily cautious in just automatically extrapolating from one to the other. Once you grasp that the Calvinistic theologies and commentaries base the great preponderance of their evidence on Old Testament rather than New Testament texts, you will start looking at their arguments in a new and entirely different light.

Our efforts are best focused on being God's evangelizing and discipling people—leaving it to God to choose when enough of God's people are meeting the conditions of His promise to unleash His blessing on their land. ⌒

Some will question whether salvation is entirely individual because the Book of the Acts of the Apostles records so many group conversions—for example, a head of the household converting and triggering the conversions of all the family members. We don't know that the family conversion happened "automatically," because the Bible doesn't state it. Scripture declares that each of us has to work out our own salvation with fear and trembling (Philippians 2:12). Since we know Scripture does not contradict itself, we have to assume that the head of the household shared the Gospel with his family who, with alacrity and joy, accepted Jesus as Savior for themselves.

God's people today comprise the New Testament church—a new entity grafted into the spiritual promises of Israel, but not heirs to the ethnic and national promises to Israel. In Ephesians chapter 2 Paul explains how the middle wall of partition between Jews and Gentiles has been broken down to make of them one new people. That's why I think it's unbiblical for converted Jews to continue to worship separately from Christians, because when they come to know Jesus as Savior they become part of the New Testament church. Now there is neither Jew nor Gentile, slave nor free, male nor female—all are one in Christ Jesus.

As a basic Bible study rule of interpretation, we have to be very careful to identify the biblical principles in the Old Testament. Such spiritual principles can be applied to the present New Testament era, but not uncritically. When we make the applications we have to point out not only the things that are the same, but the differences as well.

The Jews are still God's chosen people in a special and particular sense—Reformed, Orthodox, Conservative, or secular Zionists, genetically they are all God's chosen people. Eighty percent of the Jews in Israel are atheists or agnostics. They're still God's chosen people. Most of them went to Israel to be part of a racial homeland. They're still God's chosen people. God made certain promises to the descendents of Isaac, in belief and in unbelief. When God made promises to the entire nation of Israel, they were not conditional promises:

- "I will be their God, and they will be my people" (Jeremiah 31:33).
- "All peoples on earth will be blessed through you" (Genesis 12:3).
- "Sarah thy wife shall bear thee a son indeed; and thou shalt call his name Isaac, and I will establish my covenant with him for an ever-lasting covenant, and with his seed after him" (Genesis 17:19 KJV).

These promises were not contingent upon whether the people were believers or unbelievers, obedient or disobedient. There is no "if-then" to "I will be your God and you will be my people." There is no "if-then" to "out of your seed will all of the children of the earth be blessed." There is no "if-then" to "I will give you the land of Canaan."

How can we tell whether a promise is unconditional or conditional? By reading the Bible and recognizing the context in which it was given. Clearly, there is an "if-then" in 2 Chronicles 7:14. God's promise here is contingent upon the people's belief and righteousness.

When we are secure in our identity as God's people, we will be sure of the certainty of God's promise if we live according to our identity. During my adolescent years, I rarely left the house without hearing my mother say, "Now Richard, remember who you are." I knew exactly what she meant by that. I had been raised with a certain value system. I didn't know what to call it then, but I already had a worldview. When some yahoo was saying to me, "Hey man, c'mon, I know where we can get some beer," I had a frame of reference in place for remembering who I was, what I had been taught, and why I should remain loyal to those values.

The apostle Paul tells us that we are not our own. We have been bought with a price (see 1 Corinthians 6:20). In the Greek, the phrase is the same one used to describe purchasing a slave in order to grant him freedom. We have been purchased out of slavery to sin and into the freedom of belonging to Christ. We are in the service of the Lord—"I may never march in the infantry; I may never shoot the artillery; I may never zoom o'er the enemy; but I'm in the Lord's army."

One of America's idols is autonomy—absolute individual freedom to do whatever I want to do without someone else telling me it's wrong. The catastrophic effects of this worship of the self are all too familiar. But we in the church are under authority—gladly so. We know the tyranny of bondage to self, and so we have joyfully accepted the tremendous privilege of being called by God's name. God has given us a promise that can change America if enough of God's people heed the call to live out the Gospel in our time, shining like stars against the darkness of our culture, reflecting the sunlight of God's Son. But that starts with our willingness to be humbled—to recognize that it's God's way or no way. It's not God and country; it's God alone. Only then can God use us—His people—for His purposes in our land.

4

HUMILITY, AMERICAN STYLE

"If America would repent of her godless ways and reverse her moral decline, God would restore our moral leadership in the world and our peace and prosperity at home." Would you agree with this statement? Many of us would—it sounds right. But like many popularized opinions, it has truth as well as error.

"Well," you might ask, "what could be wrong with calling America to repent? She sure needs to do just that!"

Calling America to repentance in order to gain power abroad and more assets at home assumes that we can invoke blessing as if God is a divine vending machine just waiting to pour out benefits as soon we put the right coins in the slot. We ought to be calling others to repent in order to seek God, not to get their idea of blessing.

Another problem with this statement is that it substitutes "America" for "my people" in God's conditional promise. As we have seen, it is wrong to equate the two: the Bible certainly doesn't. Our ultimate goal is the advance of God's kingdom, not the advance of a comfortable life for all Americans.

But perhaps more subtly, this kind of thinking is quick to point the finger at others: if only *those* immoral people over there would change their ways . . . if only *those* corrupt businessmen and politicians would clean up their acts . . . if only *those* people in Hollywood would stop broadcasting such crude and godless programming . . . .

---

*O*ur ultimate goal is the advance of God's kingdom, not the advance of a comfortable life for all Americans. ◦—

Certainly we would want a stricken conscience for the immoral . . . a cleansing of corporate and government sectors for more ethical motives and practices . . . a giant step up out of the gutter for the media. But guess what is missing when our primary focus is on *them?* We have met the enemy, and they are *us.* Revival starts in the hearts of believers and spreads to unbelievers. Pride in what we think is our own righteousness is a universal characteristic of fallen human nature. But it is also a particular danger in America's self-understanding. Our unprecedented growth and success as a nation can lull us into thinking that we're entitled to what we receive because we're the right kind of people—especially for generations who haven't lived through a Great Depression or a World War with its many sacrifices.

Jesus had a few things to say about this kind of attitude. In the Sermon on the Mount, He warned against our tendency to obsess over others' sins, magnifying them while ignoring and minimizing our own (Matthew 7:3). The church has been quick to condemn the sins of our culture—and rightfully so—but slower to call Christians to repent of their accommodation to it.

AMERICAN PRIDE AND APPLE PIE

This unique brand of American pride shows itself in our "can-do" spirit, the "pull yourself up by your bootstraps" formula for success. Self-improvement is a good thing and a practical value. But especially in the American psyche, it can delude us into presuming upon God's blessing because we think we've earned it.

I think it's fair to say that fallen human beings, both regenerate and unregenerate, have a far more difficult time dealing with prosperity than they do with want. Here is God's warning to His people through Moses, recorded in Deuteronomy 6:10–12:

> When the LORD your God brings you into the
> land he swore to your fathers, to Abraham, Isaac and
> Jacob, to give you—a land with large, flourishing cities

you did not build, houses filled with all kinds of good
things you did not provide, wells you did not dig, and
vineyards and olive groves you did not plant—then
when you eat and are satisfied, be careful that you do
not forget the LORD, who brought you out of Egypt,
out of the land of slavery.

When you're in the country of the promised land, enjoying the blessings you did not earn, it's easier for you to forget the Lord your God. I think this is nowhere more true than in America. In my dad's and mom's youth, when most people still lived on farms, they understood that if it didn't rain, the crops didn't grow. If the boll weevils ate the cotton, they didn't have a harvest. But those of us in the next generation tend to think that chickens come wrapped in cellophane and milk comes from cardboard cartons, not udders. I was born after World War II, and I have no memory of the Great Depression or anything even remotely like it.

This distance from deprivation is probably even greater for my children than it is for me. We had the Cold War to contend with, the "duck and tuck" drills that were supposedly going to save us from being annihilated by a nuclear attack, and later the Vietnam War. Before the terrorist attacks on 9-11, what did my children have to deal with that was even remotely similar?

I live in a house that is bigger than the house of anybody I knew growing up. Until we started getting our children involved in volunteer programs and encouraged their schools to do so as well, they thought everybody lived in a house like theirs. They actually thought they were poor, because everybody they knew either had as much money or more money than they did.

I think Christian schools need to take the lead by requiring community service so that young people understand that not everybody has a lifestyle like theirs. I've asked my children on numerous occasions, "Exactly what is it that you did to deserve to live in this house and go to this school and live in this neighborhood?" Nothing. They just got blessed. They were conceived by the parents who brought them into the world, and these things came with the package.

I've taken my children to see the house in which I grew up. It would fit inside our garage. I'm serious! I grew up in a four-room, frame house. My brother and I lived in one bedroom, and my parents lived in the other. They were both small bedrooms. One bathroom, total. My children can't even contemplate one bathroom, or a kitchen and a living room that was also a dining room, and a one-car garage. And no air conditioning in our home until I was age fourteen, in sweltering Houston, affectionately known to natives as "sweat city."

I think it's important for my children to know that they wouldn't have it if we hadn't given it to them. We need to remind our children, and ourselves, of this when we drink from wells we didn't dig and live in houses we didn't build.

We also need to teach our children that when we dig ourselves into problems, we can't dig ourselves out in our own strength. Two contrasting statements by two of our nation's foremost leaders provide starkly opposing views of our country's troubles and how to solve them.

---

*W*hen we dig ourselves into problems, we can't dig ourselves out in our own strength. ⌒

On April 19, 1951, General Douglas MacArthur spoke to a joint session of Congress following his controversial dismissal as Commander in Chief of United Nations forces in Korea. While defending his record, he declared his opposition to war as a means of resolving international conflict, recalling his declaration aboard the battleship *Missouri* on September 2, 1945, when he formally accepted the surrender of the Japanese Empire:

> If we will not devise some greater and more equi-
> table system, our Armageddon will be at our door. The
> problem basically is theological and involves a spiritual
> recrudescence, an improvement of human character
> that will synchronize with our almost matchless
> advances in science, art, literature, and all material and

cultural developments of the past two thousand years. It must be of the spirit if we are to save the flesh.[1]

A very different assessment of America's problems was offered by then President John F. Kennedy in a speech on nuclear disarmament he gave at American University in Washington, D.C., on June 10, 1963:

> Let us examine our attitude toward peace itself. Too many of us think it is impossible. Too many think it is unreal. But that is a dangerous, defeatist belief. It leads to the conclusion that war is inevitable—that mankind is doomed—that we are gripped by forces we cannot control. We need not accept that view. Our problems are manmade—therefore, they can be solved by man. And man can be as big as he wants. No problem of human destiny is beyond human beings. Man's reason and spirit have often solved the seemingly unsolvable—and we believe they can do it again.[2]

Humbling ourselves means we agree with MacArthur, not JFK. We cannot fix our own problems, because they are illnesses of heart and soul. Our problems are not economic. They are problems of the heart. They are problems of the spirit. They are problems of the soul. Their remedies are not man-made; they are divinely ordained remedies. God alone can fix the problems that afflict our souls and our communities and our nation.

American pride and apple pie is not going to get us through our national crises. We need not dismiss our historic "can-do" spirit, but we must recognize its limits. To quote an old adage, "We need to pray as if it depended upon God and work as if it depended upon us." Without God's help, those who help themselves will come up short.

We can't "positive mental attitude" our way out of the problems we face today. We can't organize our way out of this. We can't work our way out of this. We do not have the resources. We must humble ourselves. We must rely on God.

> We can't "positive mental attitude" our way out of the problems we face today. We must rely on God. ~

We do not have the wisdom, the spiritual resources, or the strength to understand what we need to do or to muster the ability to do it. Left to ourselves, we don't know who we are and why God created us. We can't understand what God wants us to do and whom He wants us to become. We can't live the way we are supposed to live, without His help; without His guidance; without His direction. That's what it means to humble ourselves.

First Peter 5:5 tells us that God resists the proud and assists the humble. The Psalms are filled with cautions that God will not bless a proud and haughty spirit. We have every reason to be very grateful that we are Americans. This is a wonderful country. But it's wonderful because of the faith of its people and the fact that God has blessed that faith. If we credit our strength and reliance to our own resources, to the fact that we are Americans, we are doomed. "My country, love it or leave it" reflects an attitude in danger of idolizing America. God is a very jealous God. He will have no other gods before Him, even if it is a red, white, and blue one wrapped in stars and stripes.

Jesus taught us to render unto God that which is God's, and to Caesar that which is Caesar's (Matthew 22:21b). But our ultimate allegiance belongs to God. Anyone who says, "My country, right or wrong," is blaspheming. America is not our ultimate authority. Heaven help us if we ever face the situation confronting Dietrich Bonhoeffer in Nazi Germany, and we are forced to choose between obeying God and obeying America. Dietrich Bonhoeffer loved Germany as much as we love America, but he finally reached the understanding that it was God's will for him to work for the overthrow and defeat of his own country, because it was being run by a demonic person, Adolph Hitler. If obeying God means defying America, then that is the choice we must make.

ULTIMATE HUMILIATION

What does it mean to humble ourselves before God? It's not simply an act of penitence. It doesn't mean just getting down on our knees to tell God how and when we have sinned against Him. Fundamentally, humbling is an emotional and spiritual posture of helplessness before God. We are confessing to Him, "Father, our needs are far beyond our power to meet them."

The first chapter of the Gospel of John is one of the greatest gifts to us in all of Scripture. It tells us so much, so clearly, about the incarnation that we would otherwise have to labor long and hard to understand. John starts in the very first verse with a declaration of Jesus' absolute unity with the Father: "In the beginning was the Word, and the Word was with God, and the Word was God" (John 1:1). There never was a time when God was, that Jesus was not. There never was a time when God was that Jesus was not also God, and was not equal with God, and was not in close fellowship with God. But then just a few verses later he also declares, "the Word became flesh, and dwelt among us" (1:14 KJV). The incarnation: He *became.* He was always God; He became a man. He added a human nature.

Years before I joined the Ethics & Religious Liberty Commission, I taught at Criswell College in Dallas, Texas, for fourteen years. About 80 percent of my students were Southern Baptist preacher boys. Shortly after I began teaching there, I discovered that many of them really had no idea of what the Bible teaches about the person of Jesus Christ. They thought that the body, the physical part, was human, but everything else was God. That's not what the Bible says. From John we learned Jesus was God in every sense that God is God, and He became a man in every sense that we are human, except for the sin nature. He had a human soul and a human spirit. These two natures, *theos* and *anthropos,* God and human, are united in one person without any co-mingling of the two natures. If they had comingled, He wouldn't have been either fully God or fully man—just a hybrid version.

So whenever the Bible talks about the person of Jesus Christ, it can describe Him in terms of His divine nature, or it can describe Him in terms of His human nature. The Bible tells us that He is the same yesterday, today, and forever, which is what He is in His deity, or it can tell us that He grew in wisdom and stature and favor with God and man, which is what He was in His earthly humanity. That's why the writer to the Hebrews emphasizes over and over again that we don't have a high priest who can't be touched with the feeling of our infirmities. He was tempted in every way just as we are, yet He was without sin (see Hebrews 4:15).

The Bible expresses these truths about Jesus for a reason, and it isn't just so we can get our doctrine right. It's to give us the understanding that when nobody else knows how we feel, He does. When nobody else understands us, He knows what it means to be misunderstood. When people say false things about us or misjudge our motives, He knows what it means to be a target of condemnation. He knows what it means to be utterly alone.

Pride in what we think is our own righteousness is a universal characteristic of fallen human nature. ⌒

On a night when it was so cold that Peter later warmed himself by a fire (Luke 22:55), our Savior was in such agony that He literally perspired blood through the pores of His skin. We know from modern science that this is a medical phenomenon, a symptom of near-fatal stress. Jesus was in such extreme suffering that He prayed, "Father, if it be possible, let this cup pass from me. Nevertheless, not my will, but Thy will be done" (Luke 22:42).

Jesus experienced the ultimate humiliation: the abandonment of every source of help or hope on heaven and earth. He repeatedly declared that everything He did was through the Father's power, yet His agonizing journey to the cross took Him step by step into the suffering of ultimate isolation and abandonment. Because of His victory over sin and death, we don't ever have to face what He did. Because of His example, we can understand humility as the stripping away of all earthly sources of strength and power. Because this event is recorded in the Bible, we know that when we come to a place of ultimate humbling, He has been there already. And He is with us now, in our place of suffering.

If you have never experienced a Gethsemane moment, there will inevitably come a time in your life when you will. It will be a time in which no one understands how you feel: not your mom, not your dad, not your brother, not your sister, not even your spouse, and certainly not your Uncle Sam. *Nobody* is going to understand, and you will be in Gethsemane.

In this moment you will hear yourself whispering, "Father, if it is possible, let this cup pass from me." To your closest friend or loved one, you will be thinking, even if you never say it, "I never thought *you,* of all people, would fail to understand."

When that happens, Jesus understands. Hebrews 13:5 records His promise, "I will never leave thee, nor forsake thee." In that verse, there are four negatives in the Greek. We don't put negatives together in English, because that would be incorrect grammar—a double negative. This is a *quadruple* negative. The biblical writers used quadruple negatives when they *really* wanted to emphasize something. A good East Texan version of this verse would be, "I'm never gonna leave you—not never, not no-how."

---

*R*evival starts in the hearts
of believers and spreads to
unbelievers. ⌒

When you are in your Gethsemane, Jesus is there with you. When He kneels down with you to remind you of His presence, it makes all the difference when the hands extended to you are nail-scarred. He's been there. He understands. He has promised never to leave you or forsake you.

GOD WELCOMES YOUR RETURN

Jeremiah 3:12 contains a wonderful assurance of how God will respond when we humble ourselves: "Go, proclaim this message toward the north: 'Return, faithless Israel,' declares the Lord. 'I will not be angry forever.'"

One year the Southern Baptist Convention was meeting in my hometown of Houston, Texas. We were staying at the Convention hotel and we had a meeting off-site. My wife and I pulled out of the hotel and headed off down Main Street. My wife noticed that I was not driving with my characteristic velocity. Now you have to understand that my wife is not a Texan, she's a Tennessean. She has a theory that Texans do not drive their cars, they aim them, and their hood ornaments are actually scopes. So when she noticed that I was not driving in my usual Texan manner she asked, "Honey, are you sure you know where we're going?"

"Of course I know where we're going," I replied. "This is Houston. This is my hometown. I can't get lost in Houston."

It eventually became apparent—even to me—that if we kept going in the direction we were headed we would end up in Dallas instead of where we were supposed to be.

This time my wife said, "Honey, don't you think you ought to stop and ask for directions?"

"No," I answered. "I'm lost. Won't do any good to ask directions, because I don't know where I am!"

The only thing to do was to go back to the last place where I knew where I was and then ask for directions. *Return.* I had to start over again from the last place where I knew where I was. I had to return to where I lost my way.

Humbling ourselves means returning to the foot of the cross and believing the Savior who says that if we confess our sins, He is faithful and just to forgive us our sins and to cleanse us from all unrighteousness (1 John 1:9). Return and then listen to this: "Only acknowledge your guilt—you have rebelled against the LORD your God, you have scattered your favors to foreign gods under every spreading tree, and have not obeyed me,' declares the LORD" (Jeremiah 3:13).

We have to repent because getting lost is our fault, not God's. God hasn't changed.

---

*H*umbling ourselves means returning to the foot of the cross and believing the Savior who says that if we confess our sins, He is faithful and just to forgive us our sins and to cleanse us from all unrighteousness. ∽

I'm reminded of the story about the farmer and his wife who are driving to town in their truck. He's sitting there behind the steering wheel driving and she's all the way over on the other side of the cab with her elbow out the window. And they're not talking much. Finally she says, "We don't sit as close as we used to." To which the farmer replies, "I haven't moved."

Like the farmer, God hasn't moved. God has loved us, God does love us, God will always love us, and God hasn't moved. We are the ones who have moved. We've gone everyone to his own way. We're the ones who are in rebellion. We're the ones who have refused to bow and instead proclaimed, "I'm going to do what I want to do."

We *need* to humble ourselves. As Americans we have so many blessings that are nothing *but* blessings—we didn't earn them, yet we get to enjoy them. Prior to September 11, 2001, too many Americans had been finding themselves on third base and presuming they'd hit a triple.

Instead we need to bow our heads in gratitude and whisper, "Father, *thank You* for the blessing of being here. Prompt me to remember that all of this is a gift from You, and draw me to Yourself in humble obedience, for the good of our country and for the purposes of Your kingdom. In the name of Jesus I pray, Amen."

5

SEEKING GOD IN PRAYER

Early in Billy Graham's ministry, when a crisis had occurred and one of Billy's closest associates went looking for him during a break from their prayer time, he found Billy outside, lying face down in prone position. In a full suit of clothes, he had prostrated himself on the damp, dewy lawn. His face was buried in his hands, and he was pleading, "Lord, Lord, give us a word. Give us guidance. Give us direction."[1]

This is fervent prayer. This is seeking the face of God.

What we are called to in 2 Chronicles 7:14 is not presenting a list of requests to God and checking off devotions on our daily to-do list. We are summoned to spend quality time with God—that's not something we can schedule in between running errands or just before dashing out the door. It requires us to seek an audience with God.

TWO-WAY CONVERSATION

The Bible is never verbose or redundant, so whenever I see "pray" and "seek my face" side by side in the same admonition, I assume there is an intended distinction between them. In the 2 Chronicles passage, I think the emphasis in prayer is making our petitions known to God and seeking to have the Spirit pray with our spirit. The emphasis in seeking God's face is listening for His response.

> *No* one can enter into the presence of a Holy God and not be changed.

For too many Christians—and certainly this was true in my early spiritual life—praying is only a matter of us talking to God. We confess things to God and we ask Him for things: we ask for His strength, for His wisdom, for His intervention, for His instruction and guidance, for His understanding and forgiveness, for His forbearance. All of this is certainly legitimate, but mature prayer is a two-way conversation, not a monologue. It involves *listening*, letting God talk to us.

When we talk to God in prayer, we are sharing with Him as openly and honestly as we can how we truly feel and where we need help. When we are being absolutely honest with God, we discover things about ourselves that we hadn't previously known, at least not consciously.

If we lay ourselves open before God and allow the Holy Spirit to discern our innermost thoughts and motives, we'll discover areas of our lives that need touching and transforming. We will become consciously aware of our weaknesses, our jealousy of others, our insistence on holding back from God certain areas of our lives that we are reluctant to yield to His authority.

When we seek God's face, we are clearing room in our schedule, in our mind, and in our heart to listen to God. We are asking God to talk to us. We are letting God tell us who He is, why He created us, why we are the way we are, what it is He wants us to do, how we can please Him, how we can forward His kingdom, how we can do His will, how we can be God's man or God's woman on God's business in God's time with God's blessing.

Paul tells us in Romans 8 that the Holy Spirit bears witness with our spirit with groanings that cannot be uttered. This makes possible a communion that is beyond language. It is not the spiritual language of tongues, because if it can't be uttered, it's not a tongue. It is a communion between us and God in which the Holy Spirit bears witness with our spirit as believers. We discover things about our relationship with the Lord that we don't understand unless we are quiet and still and listening to the still soft voice of the Spirit and letting God pray with us and in us and through us.

Do you know the joy—and the struggle—of seeking God's face? Let Him share with you who He is. Let Him reveal to you new insights into His character. Let Him pull the veil aside and allow you to glimpse more of His plan for your life and your future. Let Him illuminate why He did not make you the same way as He did another, why you are similar to and different from your parents, why He is creating you to be the unique person He has designed you to become.

Ask God, "What is it that you want me to do?" God has a special plan and a special purpose for your life. As you seek His face and allow Him to guide you and mold you and direct you and shape you, you will gain a deeper understanding of how He knitted you together and embroidered you in your mother's womb.

OUR FATHER

Whom do you address when you pray? Does it matter, as long as you are praying in Jesus' name? If you pray to one member of the Trinity versus another, does it change the way you pray? Let's take a look at this.

When most people pray in public, even if they begin "Dear God" or "Dear Lord," they are in actuality praying to Jesus. There is nothing wrong with this, but it should not necessarily be the characteristic mode of prayer. The way Jesus taught us to pray is *to* God the Father, in the name of Jesus the Son, in the power of the Holy Spirit.

What on earth does this have to do with seeking God's face? Regardless of the terminology they use, most Christians are addressing

Jesus, at least conceptually, when they pray. They have never progressed in their understanding of who God the Father is, because they're talking to God rather than seeking His face.

The Holy Spirit does not fill a sinful vessel.

In the Gospel of John, Jesus tells us that no man has seen the Father; that God is a Spirit, and those who worship Him must worship Him in Spirit and in truth; and that those who have seen Jesus have seen the Father (John 6:46; 4:24; 14:9). The first eighteen verses of John's Gospel—as important a passage as any portion of the Bible—explain to us the relationship between the Son and the Father. In the very first verse are three phrases that cancel out every heresy the devil or the human mind has ever come up with concerning the person of Christ:

- *In the beginning was the Word.* There never was a time when God was, that Jesus was not.
- *The Word was with God.* The Word is in the closest possible fellowship with God, but is distinct. The Son is distinct from the Father.
- *The Word was God.* There is no essential difference between God the Son and God the Father; they are the same essence.

One verse, three phrases—and we have everything we need to deal with the Mormons, the Jehovah's Witnesses, anybody who makes unbiblical claims about the identity and ministry of Jesus. It's amazing that one verse could successfully defeat every Christological heresy ever concocted. All of the "was" and "is" verbs in this prologue are drawn from the same "I AM" verb God uses in the Old Testament to identify Himself.

Then when John reaches verse 14, we learn that the Word was *made* or *became* flesh. The Son was not always flesh; there was a specific time when He was incarnated. The Word dwelt among us, and we beheld His glory, the only begotten of the Father, full of grace and truth. John continues in verse 18 to explain that no one has ever seen the Father, but the only begotten of the Father has come to earth to make the Father known, to declare Him to us.

Essentially, John is saying that if we are going to know God the Father, we must come to Him through Jesus the Son. The Son literally "exegetes" the Father—meaning to bring out the truth of, to declare and interpret and explain.

In our prayer life, and far too often in our spiritual lives, our growth is stunted because we have never progressed from knowing Jesus to knowing more and more of the Father. We have not moved from a fully formed understanding of Jesus the Son to a more fully informed understanding (to the extent that is possible for finite minds) of God our Father—who sent Jesus, His Son, our Savior.

That mature understanding is critical to how we respond to God's call in 2 Chronicles 7:14, because to pray and seek His face means to understand more of who God is . . .

- in His *holiness,*
- in His *righteousness,*
- in His *sinlessness,*
- in His *omnipotence,*
- in His *omniscience,*
- in His *omnipresence.*

As this deeper knowledge of God takes root in our lives, we begin to grasp how much He really does understand . . .

- everything we *think,*
- everything we *say,*
- everything we *do.*

When this comprehension sinks into our minds and settles down into our hearts, and we hear the voice of God say "seek my face and turn from your wicked ways," then we are going to move from our wicked ways with *alacrity,* if we truly understand that someday we are all going to stand before an all-powerful, all-knowing, and ever-present God, who is a God of *righteousness,* a God of *holiness,* a God of *purity.*

To the extent that we grasp this knowledge of God, that we experience God in this way, we will not be slow to repent. We will *flee* from wickedness. We will be consumed with the fear of the Lord, in the very best sense of that term: take the shoes off your feet, because you are standing on holy ground.

No one can see the holiness of God and live. That's why God said to Moses, "I'll tell you what, Moses—I'll hide you in the cleft of a rock when I appear, and after I go by I'll let you catch a glimpse of the back side of my glory." And even at that, Moses' face shone with the reflected glow of God's *shekinah* glory.

> *To* the extent that we grasp this knowledge of God, that we experience God in this way, we will not be slow to repent. We will *flee* from wickedness.

Jesus is the manifestation of God with whom we relate. We cannot know God apart from Jesus. We cannot know the Holy Spirit apart from Jesus. Jesus is personal and intimate—but He has come to mediate not just the love of God, but also the righteousness and holiness of God. When we seek His face, we confess our sin that we might be forgiven and cleansed and filled by the Holy Spirit, moment by moment. The Holy Spirit does not fill a sinful vessel. The Holy Spirit does not fill a heart that is in rebellion, a heart that is proud, a heart that is not seeking God.

As we grasp more of the reality of God the Father, we will find it easier to turn from our wicked ways because we will be much more aware of God's righteousness and holiness.

When my oldest daughter was in the fourth grade, her school asked me to speak in chapel to the fourth, fifth, and sixth graders. I agreed to do so with great reluctance, because I have never been very good communicating with small children—including my own. Without the translation skills of my wife, I rarely communicated successfully with my children until they were about twelve years old.

A supreme example was one evening when our oldest daughter was about two and a half. I came home from work. My wife was cooking dinner, and after we greeted each other she said, "I'm just about ready to serve. Would you please tell Jennifer she needs to wash up and get ready for dinner?"

I went in and said, "Jennifer, it's time to get ready for dinner."

My daughter responded to this news by flinging her body to the floor and screaming. (It was obvious she had missed her nap that day—and of our three children, she was the one who needed it most.) So I countered with my strategy for dealing with a toddler in the middle of a temper tantrum: reasoning with her, of course.

"Oh Jennifer," I said, "how infantile!"

My mother's explanation for this cluelessness is that I suffer under a grave handicap: I was never a child. I was a miniature adult, and it was disconcerting for people to hear adult words coming out of a child's body. Later, serving as a youth evangelist while still in my teenage years, when I preached I would see twice as many adults come forward as youth.

So after I accepted the invitation to speak in chapel at my daughter's school, I thought, *What in the world am I going to say to these children?* As I prayed, God gave me a message. "God, are you *sure* this is what you want me to speak to them about?" I asked. Yes. God wanted me to speak to them about His omniscience, omnipresence, and omnipotence.

"Boys and girls," I said that day, "there are three things I want to tell you about God. First, God is omniscient."

All of the teachers rolled their eyes. *Here he goes,* they were thinking.

"What I mean by this is that God knows *everything.* Your heavenly Father knows everything that you think, everything that you say, everything that you feel, and everything that you do. Whether your parents know it or not, whether your teacher knows it or not, even whether your friends know it or not, He knows.

"Second, the Bible tells us that God is *omnipresent.* That's a big word that means God is everywhere. Not only does God know everything that you think, everything that you say, everything that you feel, and everything that you do, He is *right there with you* when you are thinking it, when you are saying it, when you are feeling it, and when you are doing it. When you hide in the closet and do something you shouldn't be doing, even if nobody else is around, God not only knows it, God is right there in the closet with you when you do it.

"And third, the Bible tells us that God is *omnipotent*. That means that God is all-powerful. So, God not only knows everything that you think, everything that you say, everything that you feel, and everything that you do; and not only is He right there beside you when you are thinking it, when you are saying it, when you are feeling it, and when you are doing it, He can do what He wants to do about it, because He is all-powerful.

"So there's no such thing as a secret from God. And God is a Holy and a righteous God, but He's also a loving and a merciful God, and that's why He sent Jesus Christ to die on the cross—so when we think things we shouldn't think, and say things we shouldn't say, and feel things we shouldn't feel, and do things we shouldn't do, God has provided a way for us to get forgiveness from Him when we're genuinely sorry. First John 1:9 says that if we confess our sins—and 'confess' means 'to say the same as,' literally, to agree with God about our sin, to agree that because of our sin, Jesus had to die on the cross, and because God loves us so much He sent His son to die for your sin and for my sin."

That may be the one sermon of mine my daughter has never forgotten. In fact, she has referenced it occasionally over the intervening years.

That's what it means to seek God's face: to understand in our bone marrow that He is omniscient, omnipresent, and omnipotent. We tend to grasp that much less and much later than we understand that He is a loving and merciful God. He *is* loving and merciful, and if we didn't grasp that we wouldn't have accepted Jesus. But I think most Christians in America today do not have a well-developed understanding of God the Father. They will get that if they pray and then listen to God, if they ask, "God, show me who You are. I'm listening. Tell me who You are; reveal Yourself to me." And then listen with the ears of the mind and the ears of the heart.

There's no such thing as a secret from God. ◦—

In our tragically broken age, many people have only negative associations to the word *father*. The answer is not to reject the concept of fatherhood, but to understand it biblically. God told us to call Him Father for good reason—obviously it tells us something about Him that He wants us to know.

However, we must be careful not to limit God's self-description to our understanding of merely human concepts of fatherhood. God does not use exclusively masculine images to describe His relationship to us. He also uses maternal metaphors. In Isaiah 49:15, He tells His people that He could no more forget them than a nursing mother could forget the baby at her breast. When Jesus lamented Jerusalem's rejection of Him, He likened Himself to a forlorn mother hen longing to gather her scattered chicks under her wings (Luke 13:34). Clearly there are aspects of God's "Godness" beyond the confines of earthly, human fatherhood. This does not in any way negate the fact that God has revealed Himself to us as our Father, and that Jesus told us to pray to Him as our "daddy" in the Lord's prayer. It does mean that even when we have exhausted all dimensions of our human understanding of fatherhood, we have not begun to exhaust who God is, as He has revealed Himself to us. Ultimately, all human descriptions of God are inadequate, because He is Spirit and He is infinite.

These maternal images do not give us license to ignore the major teaching of Scripture, which is God as Father. And Scripture reveals other dimensions of the fatherhood of God that are powerful correctives for those who lack experientially positive associations to *father.* The maternal references are supplemental to our understanding, but they are not the only ones that indicate how different our heavenly Father is from some earthly fathers.

The parable of the prodigal son (see Luke chapter 15) is the first passage I would turn to in counseling someone with this impediment. This picture of God gives the lie to distorted images such as the absentee father, the harsh and punitive father, the authority figure who is waiting to crush you for your mistakes and sins, the one who used his power as coercive force, the one who never understood and didn't seem to care all that much. The father in this story responds to his son's foolishness not by disowning him, not by a "serves him right— I knew he'd come to no good" denouncement, not by shutting him out of his life, but by scanning the horizon for his return. When a figure comes into view in the far distance, there's something familiar about it—the gait, perhaps. This father doesn't wait for his son to show up begging so he can relish the "I told you so" moment. No— he runs out ahead to greet him and swallows the boy in his embrace. And then, spares no expense for the celebration, because the son he had lost was now found.

My wife has often used narrative theology in group counseling. This is the one biblical story that everybody gets, every time. All of us want a dad like the one the prodigal son had. The good news of the Gospel is we all can have such a Father, if we accept Jesus as our Savior.

TEACH US TO PRAY

To prepare your mind and heart for a deeper understanding of God the Father, one of the best places in the Bible to start with is the Lord's Prayer (Luke 11:1–4), the prayer Jesus taught us so that we would know how to pray.

I'm sure the first time He taught this to His disciples, they didn't hear anything beyond the first few words. "When you pray, pray like this: My daddy, who lives in heaven. . . ." The word *Abba*, which Jesus used here for "father," is a term of affection, not a formal name. This was a culture in which God was so Holy they used titles to refer to Him because they dared not say His name. Yet Jesus taught them to use a word appropriate only for an intimate relationship.

Deepen your experience of God as your heavenly Father by spending some quality time with Him by praying the Lord's Prayer slowly and meaningfully, one phrase at a time, asking Him to let its truths take root in your mind and heart. Meditate on its insights into the fatherhood of God: His holiness, His power and righteousness, His provision for all our needs, His mercy and love, His guidance and protection, His glory beyond all human comprehension.

> Christians in America today do not have a well-developed understanding of God the Father.

Another passage of Scripture that can help you seek the Father is Romans chapter 8, one of the most picturesque descriptions in the Bible of our relationship to God in Christ. Verse 15 in particular affirms who we are to God: His sons. We now have the same intimate relationship with the Father, *Abba,* as Jesus the Son. We can approach God boldly because He has adopted us in Christ. He wants so much for us to come to Him in this way that He gives us the Spirit to confirm that we truly are His adopted children, and joint heirs with Christ of all the Father has given to Him. Later, in verse 23, Paul assures us that we have the "firstfruits" of the Spirit—in other words, the presence of the Holy Spirit within us is a down payment on all that is waiting for us as adopted sons of the Father now and in the hereafter.

Romans 8:26–27 gives us the assurance that even when we don't know how or what to pray, when our needs and burdens grow too great for words, the Spirit intercedes for us in groans that cannot be uttered (this is why it is an error to presume that Paul is speaking about ecstatic utterances or tongues here—there can be no speaking in tongues if there is no speaking, period). In the original Greek, the literal meaning of this statement that the Spirit helps us in our weakness is just as if we were trying to pull a telephone pole and someone came up behind us and lifted the other end. One of the New Testament words for the Spirit is *Paraclete,* or "one who is called alongside." The Holy Spirit comes alongside us, lifting our burden and carrying it with us. His intercession is so intimate that it is beyond the limitations of words. As poet Alfred Lord Tennyson wrote, "Closer is he than breathing, and nearer than hands and feet."[2]

The Father has provided all we need to come before Him, to know Him intimately, to grow in our experience of Him in all aspects of His character. But it will not happen if we harbor unconfessed sin in our hearts, if we turn away from seeking His face. It is not possible if we are living with one foot in the world and one foot in the church. Only when we humble ourselves, when we prostrate ourselves before Him, will we enter into the intimacy of His presence.

If you do this, you *will* forsake your wicked ways. No one can enter into the presence of a Holy God and not be changed. Are you willing to submit your will to His will? Are you willing to pray, "Lord, search me. Show me where my life is displeasing to You. Show me the things in my life that bring You anguish"? It is awesome and sobering to contemplate that as God's people, we can grieve the Holy Spirit. That's why the devil spends so much time tempting us, because it is the one way he can cause pain to God.

REKINDLING DESIRE

The second chapter of Jeremiah begins with exquisite tenderness:

> The word of the LORD came to me: "Go and pro-
> claim in the hearing of Jerusalem: 'I remember the
> devotion of your youth, how as a bride you loved me
> and followed me through the desert, through a land
> not sown. Israel was holy to the LORD, the firstfruits of
> his harvest. . . .'" (Jeremiah 2:1–2)

This is the language of betrothal and honeymoon. God is saying to His people, "Remember . . . remember what it was like when it was right between us."

Do you remember what it was like when you first met the one you're married to now? I do. I met my wife on my birthday—the best birthday present I ever had—in the cafeteria of the Baptist seminary in New Orleans. I tease her sometimes that we had to wait until we were in seminary to meet because she wouldn't have dated me any sooner. In high school and college she was a senior when I was a lowly sophomore, but by the time we got to seminary it didn't seem to matter that much. Greek was just a little easier and Hebrew a little more bearable when I was studying them with her; even the air in New Orleans wasn't quite as humid. Everything was better when we were together.

> When we seek God's face, we are clearing room in our schedule, in our mind, and in our heart to listen to God.

God is saying to you, "Remember what it was like when it was right between you and Me?" He says that to each of us as individuals. He says that to us in our marriages and in our families. He says that to us in our neighborhoods, in our churches, in our nation. *Remember what it was like when it was right.*

But the honeymoon didn't last, and the bride left her loved one's side, and this is what it came to: "Your wickedness will punish you; your backsliding will rebuke you. Consider then and realize how evil and bitter it is for you when you forsake the LORD your God and have no awe of me . . ." (Jeremiah 2:19). He mourns her unfaithfulness, describing her as a wild animal in heat, adulterously pursuing the fertility gods and goddesses of the Canaanites.

If "remember" evokes the past, then "consider" and "realize" (also rendered "know therefore" and "see") signify the present. God says, "Remember how it was when it was right between us, and realize it's that way no longer, and return to Me."

Isn't that what happened with David? God declared that David was a man after His own heart. When all of Israel quaked before Goliath and said he was too big to hit, David looked with the eye of faith and said he was too big to miss. I don't know about you, but I find King David to be the most frightening person in the Bible. He was a great man of God, and he should sober every last one of us, because he was living proof that if we wander away from God, yesterday's spiritual victory is no inoculation against today's spiritual defeat.

When David first laid eyes on Bathsheba, he shouldn't even have been at the palace anyway. Instead of being out with his troops where he belonged, he was living a life of idleness and luxury back at the palace. Then he started looking where he had no business looking, and he kept on looking, allowing the lust of the eye to lead to the lust of the flesh and then conspiracy to commit murder to cover up his sin.

This is the man who had braved the loneliness and peril of the Judean hills by affirming, "Yea though I walk through the valley of the shadow of death, I will fear no evil for thou art with me, thy rod and thy staff they comfort me" (Psalm 23:4 KJV). Now, as he prowls the marble halls of his palace with hundreds of servants and retainers, he's more alone than he ever was out on those Judean hills. "Oh God, forgive me," he pleads, "that the bones which thou hast broken may rejoice" (Psalm 51:8). Where do his thoughts go? "Restore to me the joy of your salvation" (v. 12). In the midst of his misery, in the midst of his brokenness, in the midst of his sin, David remembered what unbroken fellowship with God was like, and he knew it wasn't that way anymore.

Pray, and seek His face. Your heavenly Father is waiting to show you more of Himself.

6

TURNING FROM
Whose WICKED WAYS?

There is a striking picture of our world today tucked into two lines of ancient wisdom from the Book of Proverbs: "Where there is no vision, the people perish, but he that keepeth the law, happy is he" (Proverbs 29:18 KJV). The word *vision* is transliterated in Hebrew as *chazon,* meaning a message from God, the revelation of His will through His word. The word *perish* is better rendered "cast off restraint." And the *law* refers here not just to the Mosaic law, but to all of God's message to His people via His messengers. In other words, where there is no revelation, no standard, no proclamation, the people run amok—they scatter in all directions like chickens with their heads cut off.

I drive Buicks. I put about fifty thousand miles a year on them. But I don't really have a clue how they work and why. Cars are a mystery to me—I just turn the key in the ignition and drive them. I don't have to do anything else except put in the right kind of gasoline and oil. If I didn't have the maintenance manual to follow, I'd use the wrong kind and end up broken down by the side of the road, waiting for AAA to haul me to the repair shop.

We have completely ignored the owner's manual and maintenance guidelines for our lives and our marriages and our families, and we wonder why we are broken down by the side of the road. We ignore the traffic signs and wonder why the landscape is littered with accidents and traffic jams. We toss away or ignore the maps and wonder why we have lost our way.

Where there is no revelation, the people cast off all restraint. When they don't have a standard; when they don't understand that they are going to be accountable for how they live, they run amok.

A Society in Breakdown

Our society has broken down by the side of the road because it has lost a vision for who we are and why we're here. Life itself has become a means to selfish ends. God is not going to bless people who disregard the sanctity of all human life, asserting their right to kill human life because it's inconvenient. God is not going to bless a culture that permits its people to kill their own babies because it's embarrassing, or because parenthood doesn't meet their arbitrary standards for the good life. God is not going to bless a society that thinks it has the right to create life in order to kill it and harvest medicines to prolong the lives of other human beings.

God is not going to bless a society that worships mammon. I believe in capitalism because capitalism works. But men are sinful and selfish and they are not going to work productively unless they get to keep a significant amount of what they produce. But that doesn't mean we should take what *is* and enshrine it as *ought*. Just because capitalism works doesn't mean we should affirm sinfulness and selfishness. And there is a big difference between what the government should be allowed to require from us and what we should require of ourselves.

> *L*et's face it: many
> are turning away from the
> faith because they don't want
> to live by Christian
> sexual standards.

I think we need to ask ourselves as Christians in this country some serious questions about whether we should have more cars than we need to drive, more clothes than we can wear, more homes than we can live in, and more material consumption than we really need. Our society has bought into consumerism as a way of life, and it has crept from buying material things to treating others as commodities. People shop for partners who will meet their needs and gratify their desires.

Sexuality becomes a matter of consumption rather than giving and receiving in committed love, as God intended. Men pursue women as sex objects—the more the better. Predatory younger women lure older successful men away from their marriages because they see them as powerful providers in ways that men their own age are not. The pro-abortion and embryonic stem-cell research movements deny life to human persons because they are in the way or they can become useful. All of this is a form of self-idolatry: we want to do this to perpetuate our own lives, to become our own gods, to control life and death in order to gain our own immortality, or at least to postpone our own mortality as long as possible.

Our society's values used to be more reflective of biblical standards, especially in areas of personal morality. One example is cheating: according to some statistics, nearly three-quarters of all students are cheating in school—and they don't think there's anything wrong with it! We used to have a societal standard that cheating was wrong. When I was in school, cheaters were shunned. In most public schools now, if you don't do it you're considered odd.

Another example is that we have utterly lost the concept of sexual purity. We have no models of it to follow. I think this is why abstinence campaigns are striking such a nerve among young people. Teens are hungering for this kind of guidance because they have been deprived of a vision for it, and in their own peer groups they see the consequences of sexual desire run amok.

There used to be a tacitly observed public standard for moral behavior, even if it wasn't always heartfelt and internalized. If you left your wife to turn her in for a younger model, you faced a penalty of societal disapproval, often with professional consequences attached. In the 1940s and 1950s, you could lose your promotion—or even your job—if you got divorced. It was bad business. You were marginalized by the community.

Not anymore. Not unless you're a senator from Arkansas who used to be a Baptist preacher, ran on a family values platform, and then dumped your wife of thirty years to marry a young aide in your Washington office—then there's a penalty: you lose your Senate seat. Otherwise, there's not much of a price to pay. Look at former president Bill Clinton: there was plenty of uproar over whether he was lying about having an affair with a Capitol Hill intern, but after it was all said and done he didn't carry much shame for engaging in sexually illicit behavior with a young woman less than half his age. Twenty years ago, it would have been different.

First and foremost, turning from our wicked ways in this society involves living a Christian sexual lifestyle. Probably the greatest damage that is being done to the church today is through the degradation of sexuality. We live in a sexually pagan culture, in which it is far more difficult to have a healthy, mutually monogamous relationship than was the case for our parents and grandparents. In their generation, it was possible to go through a whole day without being bombarded by sexual stimuli. That's no longer possible today, unless you are unplugged from electricity and you don't get out much.

Our culture has spawned a great sexual rebellion, which has permeated the church. And this is not unrelated to doctrinal error. Let's face it: many are turning away from the faith because they don't want to live by Christian sexual standards. They are heirs of the so-called sexual revolution, and they don't want to submit to the Bible's authority on sexual practice. God will not bless a culture living a sexually pagan lifestyle that would embarrass the Canaanites.

A CHURCH IN BREAKDOWN

How have we reached a point in the church where we so closely reflect the breakdown happening in our secular culture? Part of the reason is that we live in Corinth—a sexually saturated, paganized culture that sexualizes virtually everything. Nothing in pop culture reflects Christian spirituality; we are immersed in a very difficult and spiritually hostile environment.

Here's just one example. My wife, who has a private counseling practice, was consulted by a couple in their mid-thirties who came from a pretty legalistic, works-salvation church background. Since very early in their marriage, the husband had shown little interest in sexual activity with the wife. Come to find out, he was ensnared by Internet pornography, both heterosexual and homosexual.

After the wife made this discovery, she received a call from her husband, who was attending a conference. The police had just arrested him on lewd behavior charges because of an incident in a public restroom.

She finally convinced him that they needed to see a marital counselor, so they went to the pastor of their local church. The pastor told them, "On a scale of one to ten, with ten being the worst, I would put this at about a four in terms of marital problems." When I heard this I thought, *Good grief, what's a ten?*

> ## Preachers are the calcium in the backbone of the church.

My wife had another client from a city with lots of evangelical churches and a very strong Christian community. He was on the church staff, and he was struggling to deal with his pornography addiction. Wracked by guilt and desperate for help, he finally summoned the courage to confess to the senior pastor. His pastor told him, "Oh, I have the same problem. Don't worry about it."

Oh, no.

With shepherds like this, the flock is in deep trouble.

In his new book *Bush at War,* Bob Woodward quotes President George W. Bush observing that "the president is the calcium in the backbone of the nation."[1] I'd like to add that preachers are the calcium in the backbone of the church. If the preachers don't have any moral courage, the congregations will deteriorate into spineless wonders. When there is no fidelity to preach the Word of God from the pulpit, no proclamation and understanding, the people have no vision for how to live. As Paul said when he quoted the promise in Joel 2:32 that "everyone who calls on the name of the Lord will be saved," how can the Jews call on the one they have not believed in? "And how can they believe in the one of whom they have not heard? And how can they hear without someone preaching to them?" (Romans 10:13–14). Without the revelation of the written Word and the preaching of that Word, the people run amok.

There has been a great evangelical awakening in America over the last half century. ∽

The church has a lot to answer for here: we've been good with the negatives but too often negligent with the positives. We have not taught why God endowed us with the gift of gender, why He made us male and female, why He created us as sexual beings, and how He intends for that to be expressed. We have not explained the damage that is done by not staying within these divinely ordained guidelines. If we don't teach that lesson to our children, who will?

Let's look honestly at the divorce epidemic. When the Christian community has the same divorce rate as the culture, we have no witness to the culture. I know there are bad marriages. I know there are people who, unfortunately and unknowingly, were married to those who would not keep their vows and would not reconcile and renounce their infidelity. However, it's time that we quit being plagued by "exceptionitis" and started living by the rule instead of the exception. The rule is that God hates divorce. It should not be a common phenomenon in the church.

We have not done a good job in providing premarital counseling, which can keep a lot of bad marriages from happening in the first place and help a lot of other marriages that would not otherwise survive get started on a far firmer foundation. How many times do we hear someone say, "If I had known then what I know now, I could have made it work"? Why do we *keep* hearing it? We should have made sure they knew what they needed to know, or the church shouldn't have given them its blessing by marrying them in the first place.

Some are calling for us to destigmatize divorce by acknowledging that divorce is normal. Because in fact, it is the norm. What *is,* is not what *ought.* And we are in grave danger if we accept the *status quo* as what ought to be.

A friend of mine is a religion professor at a Baptist university. Other than preparations and teaching classes, his most time-consuming and emotionally draining activity is dealing with the scores and scores and scores of Baptist young people from Baptist homes who are trying to cope with the divorces of their Baptist parents who know better but do it anyway. Making an arbitrary decision to divorce because you're unhappy and you don't want to be married anymore, or you've found a new sexual partner, or you are trying to reclaim your lost youth, or you are in a midlife crisis, is wickedness and bold rebellion against God. God is going to judge it, not bless it. It's time we understood that and acted accordingly.

SALT AND LIGHT OR SALTED AND LIT?

There has been a great evangelical awakening in America over the last half century. If you compare the state of American religion, at the end of World War II, in 1945, with the state of American religion in the first part of the twenty-first century, you see that in the last half century, America has witnessed an amazing resurgence of evangelical faith. When Jimmy Carter was running for president in the 1970s, people asked, "What's a born-again Christian?" They thought it was like a snake handler. Now, most people know what "born-again" means, whether they view it positively or negatively.

As a percentage of the population, more people consider themselves "born-again" Christians than at anytime since the Great Depression. However, we have become a nation dominated by casual Christianity. I think we have to face the fact that in spite of a widespread resurgence of evangelical "born-again" faith, the culture has influenced us more than we have influenced the culture. Instead of becoming salt and light, we have been salted and lit.

The main work that needs to be done is first in our own lives, in our own homes, in our own churches. God is not going to bless a nation in which those who claim to be "born-again Christians" do not live Christlike lives. God is not going to bless families who take their vows casually. God is not going to bless churches that fail in their responsibility to be the countercultural force for biblical holy matrimony that God intends them to be. God's blessing upon our nation will be in direct proportion to the percentage of the population of the land who are living Christlike lives that are pleasing in His sight.

Jeremiah chapter 3 addresses God's people who strayed from Him in becoming like the carnal culture of their day. But it does not simply denounce them for their sin: this passage offers a parallel promise to 2 Chronicles 7:14:

> "Return, faithless people," declares the LORD, "for
> I am your husband. I will choose you—one from a
> town and two from a clan—and bring you to Zion.
> Then I will give you shepherds after my own heart,
> who will lead you with knowledge and understanding.
> In those days, when your numbers have increased
> greatly in the land," declares the LORD, "men will no
> longer say, 'The ark of the covenant of the LORD.' It

will never enter their minds or be remembered; it will not be missed, nor will another one be made. At that time they will call Jerusalem The Throne of the LORD, and all nations will gather in Jerusalem to honor the name of the LORD. No longer will they follow the stubbornness of their evil hearts." (3:14–17)

"Return, faithless people; I will cure you of backsliding. . . ." (3:22)

Notice who does what to whom. God Himself has chosen Israel as His bride. He will provide the shepherds His people need, the knowledge and understanding they lack. When His loved ones run off and commit adultery with pagan idols, He does not divorce them. The whole Book of Hosea is a portrait of God's faithful love despite His people's unfaithfulness. The prophet's wife resumes the role of a harlot, pursuing lovers and accepting payment for her sexual favors, but Hosea pursues her nonetheless, to redeem Gomer out of her sexual slavery and restore her to a place of honor as his wife. It is clear from the text that Hosea and Gomer represent God and Israel. This potent imagery is in the Bible to show us in vivid terms how much God loves us and wants us to return to Him.

He will come after you; He will restore you. Remember what it felt like when it was right between God and you. Realize when it's not that way anymore. Turn from your wicked ways and experience the joy of God's restoration.

7

When God Hears and Responds

What kind of response can we expect from God, when we pray and seek His face and turn from our wicked ways?

Scripture does not leave us guessing about this. We can fill in plenty of detail to help illuminate what God's promise to "hear" and "respond" actually looks like in our lives. Some people struggle to overcome distorted images and anxious expectations about what God may or may not do in response to them. They have trouble believing that God truly loves them, that He will respond with mercy and love, not anger or indifference, when they approach Him in repentance, seeking His face.

God has made it very clear that He will never refuse to hear and respond to the cry of a penitent and contrite heart—as David declared in his psalm of repentance, "a broken and contrite heart, O God, you will not despise" (Psalm 51:17). God also makes it clear that He opposes the proud but gives grace to the humble.[1] Scripture assures you that when you seek His face, you will experience not only His holiness and His righteousness, His omniscience, omnipresence, and omnipotence but also His loving-kindness. No sin of yours is beyond God's forgiveness when you come with a broken and contrite heart.

GOD'S RESPONSE TO INDIVIDUALS

I was fortunate in coming to Christ at an early age. This is how I first knew God: as a loving Father who loved me enough to send Jesus to die for me—even if I were the only person on earth, He loved me enough to send Jesus to die for my sins. I came with the faith of a child. I know enough about myself that it was probably providential that I came to the Lord at a young age, because it would have been more difficult for me as an adult—as it is for most adults. By far, the largest percentage of believers is comprised of those who were converted by age twelve. The number of believers who were converted after age twelve drops off sharply, with an even sharper drop-off at age sixteen. It's a lot easier to come with the faith of a child when you're a child.

I did not get this picture of God from my relationship with my earthly father, because we were so different that it posed constant challenges to both of us. My dad worked hard, physically, all his life, and he knew and cared little for the bookish world of academics in which God allowed me to excel. My dad always loved to camp out. I looked upon each and every camping trip we took as a form of child abuse and sat behind mosquito netting reading books. I loathed it then, and the appeal escapes me to this day: Why would anyone voluntarily leave indoor plumbing and climate control? The one area of interest my dad and I shared was sports. I was an all-star in baseball and football, and that helped, but we never had the kind of relationship that allows fathers and sons to feel the intimacy that we both longed to share until I was an adult. I am grateful to God that my dad has lived long enough for us to have a better relationship in my adult years than we had in much of my childhood and adolescence. As I matured, and became a father myself, I realized my dad did the best he knew how to do, and that's all you can ask a parent to do.

The good news is, our human experience of fatherhood does not determine—or need not determine—our experience of God as Father.

My experience of God as Father started at age six, when I became a believer through a Backyard Good News Club, led by my mother. I've told friends in child evangelism, "If you want a story of a guy who stuck, I'm it." I was led to the Lord through the wordless book: "Black is the color of my sin; red is the color of Jesus' blood that cleanses me; white is what I'm washed clean as, whiter than snow; green is the color of the life I'm supposed to live for Him; gold is the color of the streets I'll walk one day." I didn't understand it all back then, but I understood enough, and it was all very vivid to me. I knew quite clearly that I wanted and needed to accept Christ. I had a profound sense of sin in general and felt convicted of my own sin in particular.

I know my experience is unusual, but I have never known a moment in my life when I didn't know that Jesus loved me, that Jesus died for me, and that Jesus had a plan for my life. That was always part of my conscious memory. It's a wonderful heritage, which my mother instilled in me, and I have never wished for a conversion experience as dramatic as some have had.

At six I knew Jesus died for me and wanted to live in my heart, and I asked Him to save me and forgive my sin and come to live in my heart forever, and He did.

However, I do know that some people rarely have known a moment in their lives when they were absolutely convinced that Jesus loved them, died for them, and had a plan for their life. Most people go through some significant phase of doubt and questioning, especially while in college; and some struggle with it all their lives. I have never doubted once since my conversion.

This has given me a tremendous sense that all God's blessings are unearned. Some Christians get on third base and think they hit a triple. I know I didn't—God always helped me run the bases. It's only God's mercy and grace, not anything special in me, that accounts for my virtually lifelong assurance of God's saving presence in my life.

The good news is, our human experience of fatherhood does not determine—or need not determine—our experience of God as Father. The Word of God provides the truth we can stand on. As we pray and seek God's face, He will open our minds and hearts to His Word so that it takes hold in our lives. When we humble ourselves and seek God in repentance and prayer, we can be confident that He hears us and that He will respond to us in mercy and grace.

God's Response to a Nation

God's people are individual believers, joined in congregations. The 2 Chronicles 7:14 promise is made to believers, but when God responds with blessings, they can extend beyond individuals to an entire society or nation.

Forgiving sin is a blessing for individuals, specific to believers. But healing the land includes everybody. If the righteous pray for rain and the drought ends, the unrighteous are blessed as well. When the locusts descend on believers and unbelievers alike, everyone suffers. If

God gets rid of the locusts, everybody's crops benefit. Jesus instructed us to love those who oppose our faith, "that you may be sons of your Father in heaven. He causes his sun to rise on the evil and the good, and sends rain on the righteous and the unrighteous. If you love those who love you, what reward will you get? Are not even the tax collectors doing that?" (Matthew 5:44).

Of course, the unrighteous or unbelievers are not blessed eternally, and their blessings here on earth are indirect, but they do share in the blessing that is extended to the nation. Because of the repentance, prayer, and righteous lives of Christians, non-Christians benefit. The good crops grow in the fields of just and unjust alike.

Even when unbelievers think they don't want God's blessing, they still benefit. Would they be blessed by a society in which biblical sexual mores were the norm? Yes, they would be blessed, in spite of themselves. The actions of a few can bring healing to an entire nation.

Is America under Blessing or Judgment?

There is a lot of contention among Christians about whether America is blessed or judged, and what constitutes evidence of blessing or judgment. I think there are many signs of God's blessings on America as a nation, in spite of all our faults, for the ways in which at least a portion of our population has been obedient.

For example, I don't know of another country in which a child born into my circumstances, the son of a welder and a homemaker, could get an academic scholarship to Princeton University and then a graduate education at Oxford University. Or where else in the world could a seventeen-year-old German Jewish refugee immigrate and climb the ranks to a powerful cabinet position with global influence, as Henry Kissinger did when he became secretary of state under Richard Nixon and won the Nobel Peace Prize?

I look at the United States of America, and I see many signs of God having blessed us in many ways that He has not blessed other countries. That blessing has fallen on the just and the unjust, just like the judgment falls on the just and the unjust. There were many righteous Gentiles who hid Jews from the Germans, but they still had their country bombed flat, divided in two, and their women violated by the Red Army when it captured Berlin.

Jerry Falwell and Pat Robertson tried to imply that the terrorist attacks on America were God's judgment on this country because of homosexuals and abortionists. But passages such as "If my people who are called by my name . . ." or "the Lord disciplines those he loves, and he punishes everyone he accepts as a son" (Hebrews 12:6), in which God talks to the righteous, suggest otherwise.

If more Christians had been living righteously, is it possible that the devastation of September 11 could have been minimized?

That terrorists might not have succeeded in their plans? That the CIA and FBI would have been more effective in their intelligence-gathering, more proactive?

That's an impossible question to answer, but it's worth thinking about. Consider the arrests of sniper suspects in the Washington, D.C., area after several weeks of terror left ten dead and three injured. Truck driver Ron Lantz spotted the suspicious car at an Interstate rest stop, and he and another trucker blocked the exit with their trailers until police arrived. Not widely reported was that a week earlier Lantz had gathered fifty other truck drivers to pray for "America, for an end to evil in our country, and for an arrest of the snipers."[2] God hears the prayers of a righteous man. That event seems to have been a sign of God's blessing.

If we look at national disasters as incidents of God's judgment, it's more likely they are directed toward reprobate and unrepentant believers in this country than the unsaved and unregenerate. We have to be hesitant, however, in jumping to assumptions that events such as September 11 are acts of God's judgment. If it was a sign of God's judgment and He allowed it to happen, it's more a judgment on believers in this country—those who are part of the 40 percent claiming to be "born-again Christians," according to Barna's Research, but not the 14 percent who are trying to live their lives according to the moral and ethical teachings of Scripture.

Are We Experiencing Spiritual Revival?

I think it's very possible that there is a spiritual revival going on in America. But I could also cite compelling evidence that we are reprobate people. Probably both are true, but my guess is that there are now more born-again, true-blue Christians as a percentage of the population than at any other time since the early twentieth century. This seems clear from the increasing number of people who claim to be born again, the rise of the evangelical movement in the last fifty years, and the growth of evangelical churches.

However, those who aren't Christians have no reason not to go out and live like the devil, so many of them are living like pagans. The sad reality is that many of those who claim to be born again are not living any differently than the culture around them.

Before the Civil War, Protestant Christianity constituted the moral authority for society. There were some blind spots—race and women chief among them. The ministers were considered the cultural leaders of the community, and the churches were the social arbiters. That ended, at least in the North, after the Civil War, with a radical shift from pastors and churches to business leaders being the social leaders of the community, in the half century from the end of the Civil War to the beginning of the World War I. That didn't happen as much in the South, so the South became the Bible Belt, but the South didn't count nationally in terms of the cultural authority because it was conquered territory, with very exotic and often sinful folkways such as segregation, Jim Crow, and lynchings.

The belief that we could treat blacks differently, and the belief that women should not have equality as citizens were both wrong and sinful. Those were clearly the two big blind spots for American Christianity, perhaps even Western Christianity, from the Reformation until the modern era. I came as a teenager into the turmoil of the Civil Rights Movement of the 1960s. I'm grateful to God that I was always raised in a home where I was taught that racism not only was wrong, it was sinful. It was a rebellion against God's will, and we've seen the law rightly change behavior. But only the Gospel can change attitudes, beliefs, and hearts, and that's why the most segregated moment in American life is still Sunday morning, and that is a reproach to the Gospel of Jesus Christ.

BLESSING, JUDGMENT, OR NATURAL OCCURRENCE?

Blessing is God's favor—God making positive and good things happen. The alternative to blessing is judgment. A land that God blesses is not overrun with twenty-plus sexually transmitted diseases at epidemic levels because of the people's immorality. Some argue over whether this is God's judgment or a naturally occurring consequence of immorality. I'm not sure the two are all that different. God never intended for us to be promiscuous. To the extent that we are, we will suffer consequences. Is sclerosis of the liver a divine judgment? Well, God never intended for us to booze it up. There are natural consequences of boozing it up—to name just one, it will kill your liver.

God created us. He knows how we work and how we don't work. Men who dump their first wives and marry younger women die almost ten years earlier than men who remain married to the wife of their youth. Is that a judgment by God? Not directly, but when we break God's laws, they break us.

> *My* guess is that there are more "born-again," true-blue Christians as a percentage of the U.S. population than at any other time since the early twentieth century. ⌁

If I step out of a twenty-story building, I don't break the law of gravity; it breaks me. Is that God's judgment? Not directly. It is indirectly, in the sense that God has laid out rules and proscribed behaviors and when we sever His boundaries, there are natural consequences—which may be enhanced by specific judgments.

Is AIDS a judgment of God on homosexuality and sexual immorality? Not directly, but there are few male homosexuals living an active homosexual lifestyle who don't have a suppressed immune system. God never intended for us to have scores of sexual partners in casual encounters. That's going to suppress anyone's immune system.

When we behave in ways God never intended for us to behave there are going to be consequences. I would certainly never say that AIDS was a direct judgment of God. But I would put it right up there as a natural consequence of breaking God's rules, along with sclerosis of the liver, lung cancer from smoking, syphilis, gonorrhea, and herpes. Twenty percent of the adult population has genital herpes, an incurable sexually transmitted disease.

Think about having to confide in the person you hope is going to be your future spouse, "Honey, there's something I need to tell you. Because of some unfortunate lifestyle choices I made in the past, I have genital herpes." That's not a conversation I'd really want to have. But 20 percent of the adult population will have to—or should—if they are contemplating marriage. If they don't they're not laying the basis for a sound and honest relationship.

What do God's blessing and judgment look like? We can see from the Old Testament what it meant for Israel: material prosperity in crops and herds and God's protection against enemies, or failure of crops and herds and the subjugation of the people to the conquering Babylonians and Assyrians.

What do they, or will they, look like for America? Let's envision what a bright future might look like when enough of God's people unite and bring blessing upon their land.

8

THE PERSON GOD WILL BLESS

Consider a man who helped bring revival in his time. He and his fellow countrymen had been exiled in a far country after another nation took them captive. After a regime change among their captors, they were allowed to return to their homeland. What happened next testifies to the power of prayer, the authority of God's Word, and the difference it can make when one man takes a stand for the Lord in his society.

The story is chronicled in the Book of Ezra. There are many parallels between Ezra's time and our own. Ezra was called to serve God when his people were returning to a destroyed homeland. All of the walls were down, and they needed rebuilding—just as we must rebuild the walls of our society in restoring what has been destroyed by the advance of secularism.

The Scripture records the moment of Ezra's return, after a tiring journey of many months: "Ezra arrived in Jerusalem in the fifth month of the seventh year of the king. He had begun his journey from Babylon on the first day of the first month, and he arrived in Jerusalem on the first day of the fifth month, for the gracious hand of his God was on him" (Ezra 7:8–9). Whenever Scripture uses the anthropomorphism of God's hand, it signifies blessing and power. When my wife wants to make me feel like I'm the great provider, she will say to me, "I can't get this jar of peanut butter open. Would you please open it for me?" Only too happy to comply, I take the jar and—open it with my teeth? Put it under my arm? No, I use my hand. I apply the power that I have to my hand, and I open the peanut butter jar and return it in quiet triumph to my wife.

> The person God blesses is growing in his or her knowledge of God and applying that knowledge in becoming more Christlike. It's not enough just to know it; we have to *live* it.

The hand is power applied. Ezra knew what it was to be God's person in God's place, at God's appointed time, on God's business, through God's power, with God's blessing. How on earth did he do that—was he just lucky to get picked to be a biblical hero? Scripture tells us in Ezra 7:10: "For Ezra had devoted himself to the study and observance of the Law of the LORD, and to teaching its decrees and laws in Israel."

Ezra was a scribe and had an enviable reputation for being a Scripture expert. But he didn't simply accumulate knowledge of the Scriptures so he could be a walking reference book. Some of us are content simply to know more about the Bible than anybody else in church. But Ezra "devoted" himself, or the King James renders it "prepared his heart"—this means that he made it the goal and purpose of his life to know, live, and teach the Law of the Lord. Never fall into the trap of a fearless familiarity with holy things. There is more in the Bible than you can ever learn in your lifetime. Don't ever lose your awe at the holy things of God. The person God will bless is devoted to understanding and applying God's Word with a holy reverence.

THE WAR WITHIN

Too often as Christians we presume we're doing fine—if only the rest of America would turn back to God, we could get this country back on the road to righteousness. But God's words in 2 Chronicles 7:14 are not addressed to a pagan culture. They are addressed to His people. We live in a sinful culture that brazenly practices wicked ways, and we have assimilated many of them. Turning the tide towards God's blessing doesn't start with our pagan culture. It starts with the saved:

paganized Christians who choose to seek their heavenly Father and turn from the wicked ways that have led them astray. The word *revival* is an interesting word. In order to be revived, you have to have been "vived" already at some time in the past. Great movements of God always start with God's people getting right with God.

When we accept Jesus as Savior, we're no longer enslaved to our sin nature, but we don't lose it. We now have two natures, fighting for control. My grandmother used to say it's like two dogs in a fight: the winner will be the one you feed the most. How do we feed our Christlike nature? By humbling ourselves, praying and seeking His face, and turning from our wicked ways. How do we feed the carnal nature? By *not* humbling ourselves, *not* praying and seeking His face, and *not* turning from our wicked ways.

If evangelical Christians today have a blind spot, it's our woeful neglect that the sin nature is alive and well and always looking to enlarge its turf in our lives and hearts. We need to remind ourselves daily that we are in a spiritual warfare—a warfare that is often more intense from within than it is from without. "The heart is deceitful above all things," warned the prophet, "and beyond cure. Who can understand it?" (Jeremiah 17:9). The original Hebrew carries the connotation that the wickedness of the heart is revealed precisely at the point of thinking, *I'm not so bad . . . at least I'm not as bad as So-and-So.* In fact, the question is not whether I am as bad as So-and-So, because I can always find somebody worse than I am. The real question is, Am I as good as I should be? And the answer is always no, because the standard is Christ. That should be our daily goal—to be more Christlike.

Knowledge of God needs to move from head to heart to extremities, from belief to obedience, from orthodoxy to orthopraxy. God does not expect us to be superachievers, but He does expect us to be growing in grace. He does expect us to apply our knowledge today more than we did yesterday. Paul told the Corinthians in chapter 3 of his first Corinthian epistle that he had to treat them like spiritual babies because they were still carnal. They had to be started on milk because they weren't ready for meat. It's okay to be a baby when you're a baby, but at some point it's time to move on from the bottle to solid food.

Despite the growth of evangelical churches, there is a widespread pattern today of spiritually arrested development: people who are ignorant of large swaths of God's Word; who base their relationship with God on feelings and experience alone; who are preoccupied with themselves instead of serving others; who attend church to be fed instead of to feed.

God says we are to hide His word in our hearts that we might not sin against Him (see Psalm 119:11). The person God blesses is growing in his or her knowledge of God and applying that knowledge in becoming more Christlike. It's not enough just to know it; we have to *live* it.

We obstruct God's blessing in our lives by *not* doing what God tells us to do. Those who are obedient are in a position to receive God's blessings. Those who are disobedient can expect to receive judgment. In this sense, judgment means chastisement—it is not related to salvation. Salvation is eternal and unconditional. If you accept Jesus Christ as your personal Savior, you are saved for eternity. But blessing is conditional: its promise is upon behavior and performance. God is faithful to give us the ability to do whatever He asks of us.

*D*espite the growth of evangelical churches, there is a widespread pattern today of spiritually arrested development. ⌒

God will not bless us as believers when we know to do good and don't do it; when we know not to do evil and do it anyway. We are judged more harshly than the world, because the world acts out of ignorance. Unbelievers face eternal judgment, from which we have been delivered by trusting in Jesus Christ as Lord and Savior. The Bible tells us that God chastises those who are His children.

How do we square the conditional promise of blessing with the concept of grace in the Christian life? First, the Bible is very clear that our salvation is based on grace: free, unmerited favor. This is a permanent condition once we accept Jesus as Lord and Savior. Second, the conditions that place us in positions of blessing or chastisement are part of our sanctification. The process of sanctification is conditional, and it changes from moment to moment and day to day. The Lord has made it clear that those who choose to live however they want, knowing that they are sinning against the grace of God, are committing the sin of presumption.

The Bible is clear in Hebrews 12:5–11 that God disciplines His beloved children. In 1 Corinthians chapter 11, Paul indicates that believers face consequences of physical illness and death for coming to the Lord's table in an unworthy manner, with unconfessed sin in their hearts. Another example of judgment on believers is Paul's instruction in 1 Corinthians 5:1–5 to expel unrepentant members of the church involved in sexual sin that even pagans don't commit—a man in relationship with his stepmother, or perhaps even worse, his natural mother. It's clear that although the sinner faces censure and possibly even physical destruction, he will not lose his salvation. That's grace.

When we receive salvation, we lay a permanent, immovable foundation. How we live as believers determines whether we build on that foundation in ways that have eternal value or will eventually prove futile:

> By the grace God has given me, I laid a foundation
> as an expert builder, and someone else is building on
> it. But each one should be careful how he builds. For

no one can lay any foundation other than the one
already laid, which is Jesus Christ. If any man builds
on this foundation using gold, silver, costly stones,
wood, hay or straw, his work will be shown for what it
is, because the Day will bring it to light. It will be
revealed with fire, and the fire will test the quality of
each man's work. If what he has built survives, he will
receive his reward. If it is burned up, he will suffer loss;
he himself will be saved, but only as one escaping
through the flames. (1 Corinthians 3:10–15)

Those who build unworthily will still be saved, but they won't get any
rewards at the judgment of believers' works. Our salvation is by grace
alone, but that does not mean that law is turned into license.
Receiving God's blessings between coming to salvation and going to
our eternal home depends entirely upon our obedience: (1) humbling
ourselves, because God does not bless a proud and haughty spirit; and
(2) praying, seeking His face, and turning from our wicked ways. To
the extent that we do that, we invoke God's blessings. To the extent we
don't do that, we invoke God's judgment.

This does not mean that we are saved by grace and sanctified by
works. We are sanctified as we grow in grace and become more
Christlike. Grace is what enables us to grow. We will be more likely to
humble ourselves, to pray, to seek God's face, to make sure we don't
have unconfessed sin in our lives. But it's not enough to say, "God,

make me what You want me to be," and then go off and do whatever we want. It's going to be pretty hard for God to make you into what He wants you to be if you're looking at lewdness on the Internet or filling your mind and heart with sinful thoughts and desires. But if you seek His grace to grow in Christ, God will empower you to become the kind of person He blesses.

THE MAN, THE WOMAN GOD WILL BLESS

Now I'd like to look more specifically at how each of us becomes the man God will bless or the woman God will bless. What does blessing look like in believers' lives as husbands and fathers, wives and mothers? God gives the gift of celibacy to some, but that is the exception rather than the rule. To understand God's purpose in creating human beings as male and female, we need to start with their creation:

> Then God said, "Let us make man in our image,
> in our likeness, and let them rule over the fish of the
> sea and the birds of the air, over the livestock, over all
> the earth, and over all the creatures that move along
> the ground." So God created man in his own image, in
> the image of God he created him; male and female he
> created them. God blessed them and said to them, "Be
> fruitful and increase in number; fill the earth and sub-
> due it. Rule over the fish of the sea and the birds of

the air and over every living creature that moves on the ground." (Genesis 1:26–27)

The man and the woman together have dominion over the earth. They were created in God's image, clearly distinguishing human beings as different in kind from the rest of creation. There is a fire wall between human beings and the rest of creation. We are not just the most sophisticated and highly evolved beings on the evolutionary scale. We are the only beings created in the image of God. Although that image is marred by the Fall, it is still the *imago dei*. It is not obliterated. We are not successors to the chimpanzee, allegedly our closest relative according to evolutionists (although sometimes human behavior descends so low I find myself questioning the distinction).

God said it is not good for man to be alone. Marriage is the dominant state He intends for most people, in most places, at most times. The man or woman God will bless is first and foremost sexually pure, living either a celibate lifestyle as a single or a monogamous lifestyle as a spouse.

There are different parts of the Bible that have particular relevance for aspects of Christian doctrine in the history of the Christian faith. For example, Romans and Galatians were critically relevant at the time of the Reformation for recovering the understanding that we are saved by grace through faith, not by works. If these two books were key for the sixteenth and seventeenth centuries, then I would posit that the most relevant books of the Bible for our time are 1 Corinthians and Song of Solomon, in that order. This is because essentially, we live in Corinth.

Corinth was the sexual cesspool of the Roman Empire. The Romans, who could by no means lay claim to sexual propriety, considered the Corinthians degenerates. They made jokes and caustic remarks about Corinth. They even had a saying that if someone had become (by Roman standards) hopelessly debauched, "Well, Marcus has been Corinthianized." This is the degraded civilization in which early Christians learned to follow Christ, and Paul made very clear how they were to come out and be separate from it:

> Do you not know that the wicked will not
> inherit the kingdom of God? Do not be deceived:
> Neither the sexually immoral nor idolaters nor
> adulterers nor male prostitutes nor homosexual
> offenders nor thieves nor the greedy nor drunkards
> nor slanderers nor swindlers will inherit the kingdom
> of God. And that is what some of you were. But you
> were washed, you were sanctified, you were justified
> in the name of the Lord Jesus Christ and by the Spirit
> of our God. (1 Corinthians 6:9–11)

Don't let anyone tell you that sex is a natural expression of feelings and appropriate for any two consenting individuals, that there's nothing wrong with having multiple sexual partners, that homosexuals are made that way and can't change. The Bible says there were people in those lifestyles in Corinth who were changed by the blood of Jesus Christ.

GENDER MATTERS

I often say that a good starting point for the America God will bless would be in the 1950s, minus the racism and the discrimination against women of that time. However, although women have been granted full equality—and rightfully so—are they better off now than they were then? I think I could make a convincing argument that they are not.

In the 1950s, a woman wasn't being physically assaulted every nine seconds. She is today, most often because she is living with a man to whom she is not married. Were women abandoned by their husbands with social impunity then, the way they are now? No. Were women raped and treated with such sexual disrespect in real life and in the media then, to the extent they are today? No.

I am not trying to defend discrimination against women, but I'm not sure that women still, in spite of that discrimination, weren't better off fifty years ago in terms of their place in society, their physical safety, and their expectations that the men in their lives would keep the commitments they made to them. Some of the trouble we have today is that philosophies such as sexual freedom, or the idea that men and women aren't any different, have traveled along with the drive for sexual equality.

In a conference on sex and marriage at which I was speaking, I shared the platform with a secular guidance counselor at a community college. According to this counselor, the girls she deals with are always so frustrated and disillusioned in their relationships with boys. They want sex to *mean* something.

Let's just say it straight. In their fallen state, men are different from women in that men give love and commitment to get sex, and women give sex to get love and commitment. This is a bit of an oversimplification, but all generalizations have a kernel of truth. And when women give sex without requiring love and commitment, carnal men are going to take it, no questions asked. As my East Texas grandmother would say, "When you are handing out free milk, who is going to buy the cow?" It's illustrated in the picture of a man and woman going to a hotel for an afternoon of illicit sexual pleasure. On the way in, she trips over the door sill and he says, "Oh, are you OK, babe? Did you hurt yourself?" On the way out, she trips over the door sill and he says, "Clumsy, aren't you?" It's not a pretty picture.

A fallen man's sexual fantasy is to have sex with many different women partners. A woman's—as I am told—is to have an exclusive sexual relationship in a mutually fulfilling commitment that involves love, tenderness, and emotional intimacy. For a woman to experience that fantasy, men must be willing to say, "I love you enough to give up my fantasy." When women don't require that, the sexual revolution is far more liberating for men than it is for women, because the results of sexually irresponsible behavior are entirely different for men than they are for women—that's just biological reality. Women are the ones who get pregnant. This has nothing to do with society arbitrarily assigning gender responsibilities. And fallen men are much more capable of engaging in emotionally unrelated sexual activity than women. Our society permits them to indulge in extremely irresponsible sexual behavior without consequences.

> Never fall into the trap of
> a fearless familiarity with
> holy things.

For women, the damaging consequences of sexual freedom are social as well as biological. After divorce, 70 percent of the time men's standards of living go up while women's go down. That didn't happen a few decades ago, when guys were living in garage apartments trying to pay alimony. No-fault divorce has been no-win for women. The whole sexual liberation movement has been a very bad bargain for women, and a very good one for men who want to behave irresponsibly.

The husband God will bless and the wife God will bless are in a monogamous relationship of lifetime commitment within the sanctity of marriage. What about those who never married, and those whose

THE PERSON GOD WILL BLESS

marriages were broken through immorality and abandonment? What does a life of blessing look like for them?

THE SINGLE PERSON GOD WILL BLESS

In medieval times, the Christian faith went off track because it celebrated an ideal that those who were celibate and living a monastic lifestyle were more holy and Christlike than people who were married. The Protestant Reformation rightly corrected this distortion, as Martin Luther led the way by leaving the monastery and marrying a nun. That was a pretty dramatic statement that marriage is a holy state and that the celibate lifestyle is not elevated above it.

Unfortunately, too often today we have done exactly the opposite. We have relegated people in the single lifestyle to a second-class spiritual citizenship. Paul's discourse on marriage in 1 Corinthians chapter 7 clearly establishes the legitimacy of singlehood. God has ordained it for some people. Particularly those of us who follow Jesus Christ, who was after all single, must acknowledge celibacy as a perfectly acceptable and honorable alternative to the norm for most people.

There are others who, through no choice of their own, find themselves single through loss of a spouse or because of a partner's rebellion and unfaithfulness. Today, we are dealing with more single people in the church than ever before. As fellow Christians, we have no business looking at single people as if they are in waiting for the cure of marriage. What God said to Ezra was true for the Jews and it is true for all of us—no matter what our circumstances, if we are committed to obedience then God will bless us and God will use us, because God is sufficient.

You may have found yourself in a situation where through no fault of your own, you are a single father who is not living with his children. How can you be the father God will bless? Put God first and put your children above yourself. Seek to live before them what it means to be a godly father. Just because you are not living in the home does not relieve you of the obligation or the opportunity to have a role in their lives. Never, ever criticize their mother, even if she is eminently criticizable. Never, ever talk about your sexual relationship with the other parent or anyone else. That's emotional child abuse and can be very damaging. Even if you know your wife was running around with somebody while you were out making a living, she is still their mother, and treating her with respect is part of your responsibility to provide a godly father figure for your children.

For a divorced woman, I would say the same thing. However tempting it might be, don't criticize their father. Unless he is dangerous or in a lifestyle beyond redemption, do what you can to encourage him to have a role in the children's lives. No one else can really be their father in the way he can, if he wants to be and chooses to be.

Be encouraged by the lives of women throughout history who became single parents because their husbands died young. Mary the mother of Jesus might be a good example. Joseph was probably a good bit older than Mary when they got married, given the customs of the time, and most likely died while she was still relatively young. Some speculate that Jesus didn't start His earthly ministry until he was thirty because he was taking care of the family. We don't know that, but it would easily fit the demographics of the time period.

The lives of exemplary single moms show that others went through the same struggles you face, and they made it. You know God is sufficient. Is it easy? No. Would it be better to have a healthy two-parent home for your children? Sure. But there is a difference between not having a husband and thinking you just don't need one. There is a difference between your children having an absentee father and you thinking they don't need a father.

If you are a divorced man or woman or a single dad or mom, I want to acknowledge your reality and encourage you even though you no longer find yourself in God's desired plan for a faithful marriage and a two-parent family. Don't be discouraged. You can become the divorced person or single parent God will bless.

THE CHRISTIAN GOD WILL BLESS

Those of us who have been Christians for many years can run into the danger of becoming smug about our perseverance in the faith. We're proud of our insider status, and we start thinking we deserve better treatment than the reprobate because we have kept the faith while they were messing up right and left.

In the parable of the prodigal son (see Luke chapter 15), most of us identify with the prodigal, regardless of whether our rebellion has been as outward and extensive as his. But who is the elder brother? Sometimes, it's the church.

Think of those who brought to Jesus the woman caught in adultery (John 8:3–5). "Wait a minute: you're *forgiving* this promiscuous woman and making her clean? You mean, we're supposed to treat this blatant sinner the same way as we would a woman who has kept the law?" What do you mean, you're celebrating this prostitute coming to Jesus when nobody ever celebrated me keeping my virginity until I got married?

The believer God will bless is not the one who acts the part of the elder son, feeling superior to the lost, resenting God's forgiveness of other family members who have fallen into temptation, demanding that others get the treatment they deserve.

When I was asked to speak at a remembrance on the first anniversary of the attack on America on September 11, 2001, I reflected on what those people who had perished would say to us if they could. I think they would ask this question: "Are you ready?"

Those of us who are living in the United States of America are blessed so richly it's beyond our ability to describe or really, completely comprehend.

I think about having been born in the first flush of recovery after World War II, and the life I have been privileged to live in this country. It would be nice to say that I just happened to pick the right place and time, but that's not how it works. I enjoy blessings due to providential circumstances over which I've had no control.

Whenever I go anywhere close to my hometown of Houston, I make my way to Goode's Barbecue on Kirby Drive for unbelievable barbecue, unbelievable jalapeño cheese bread, and unbelievable pecan pie. They have a memorial there to Great Barbecuers of history and The Texas Hall of Flame and Museum of Chili Culture. I have a T-shirt I got there, which their staff all wear, that says "Goode's Barbecue and Hall of Flame" on the front. On the back is written, "I don't know about you, but I think you ought to give some thought to thanking your lucky stars that you live in Texas." Just so, I think we all ought to give thanks to God Almighty that we live in this great and wonderfully blessed land.

At the 9-11 anniversary remembrance, "Taps" was played. Every time I hear that beautiful and mournful tune I am reminded of a historic funeral for a man I greatly admire, Sir Winston Churchill. As prime minister of Britain he led his nation to stand alone for more than a year under savage attack from Nazi Germany. Churchill's funeral was held in state at St. Paul's Cathedral in London and drew leaders from around the world to pay respects to a man whose courage and strength led his nation from despair to triumph and whose influence had spread worldwide. In addition to classic church hymns and Anglican liturgy, Churchill had specifically requested that at the conclusion of the funeral liturgy, a bugler be positioned in the dome of the cathedral to play the musical salute, "Taps." There was a dramatic pause immediately following, and then bursting into the silence from across the dome was a second bugle call playing "Reveille," the staccato notes for "It's time to get up; it's time to get up; it's time to get up in the morning."

That was a tremendous testimony that death is not the end, but is swallowed up in victory for those who have a saving relationship with Jesus Christ. Life can end in a moment, and we are not in control, but God is. As our nation confronts evils attacking from without and undermining from within, we can stand up in confidence to ask God for the grace to become the individuals God will bless, that He might bring blessing to this entire country through His people. Second Chronicles 7:14 can become our "Reveille"—it's time to stand up; it's time to stand up. Are you ready?

9

THE FAMILY GOD WILL BLESS

There are three and only three divinely ordained institutions in human society, each with its proper and appointed sphere. First and foremost, there is the home: the family ordained by God. The second is the church, and the third is the government. As Christians, we all have responsibilities in each of these three institutions. Everything goes well when these three spheres are operating in harmony as God intended. Problems arise when one of those spheres begins to lean on or overlap another.

For example, the Bible says that parents have the responsibility to raise children in the nurture and admonition of the Lord. It doesn't say anything about the government raising children in the nurture and admonition of the Lord. The primary responsibility for raising your children is in your hands, not the government's, and when the government starts putting it's hand into your family's sphere you need to slap that hand, and if it doesn't stop, slap its face.

God has a certain place that He wants the home and the family to have in human society, and He has not left us clueless about our family obligations and responsibilities. In the home, our responsibilities are first of all as children, to honor our parents. Then we have responsibilities within marriage to our spouse. If and when we have children we take on responsibilities as parents, for which God holds us accountable. Singles have responsibilities as extended family members, and to support, rather than undermine, married couples.

Too often government has tried, or in many cases been forced by neglect, to take over the functions which God intended for the family. ⟋

The family God will bless comprises a man who is being the husband, father, and spiritual leader God wants him to be and a woman who is being the wife, mother, and godly woman God wants her to be. They raise their children in the nurture and admonition of the Lord. And part of their raising their children in the nurture and admonition of the Lord is providing a spiritual home for them in a local church.

One of the great difficulties of the last half of the twentieth century in the U.S. is that too often government has tried, or in many cases has been forced by neglect, to take over the functions which God intended for the family and those which God intended as the responsibility of the church. Since the family is the foundational building block institution for all of human society, that's where we need to start in creating the conditions of God's promise in 2 Chronicles 7:14.

IT TAKES TWO TO BE COMPLETE

The second chapter of Genesis records God's creation of man and woman, and His design for the life that man and woman will share in together: "And the LORD God said it is not good that man should be alone. I will make him a helpmeet for him" (2:18 KJV). God's declamation here is not the ordinary, routine neutral expression of displeasure. It is the strongest usage available in the Hebrew language to express a negative reaction. Even before sin entered the world, it was bad for man to be alone.

God has revealed Himself in the Trinity to be a God of fellowship, and in relationship to His people a God who desires fellowship with His creatures. By creating us in His image, He imparted that relational dimension to us as human beings. We are meant to be in fellowship with each other; it is "not good" for us to be alone. This is a very strong negative, particularly when it is contrasted with the strong positives that have gone before it. A recent study compiled by a panel of leading children's doctors, research scientists, and youth service professionals entitled *Hardwired to Connect: The New Scientific Case for Authoritative Communities* confirms that God created us to connect with one another and this intention can be traced "in the basic structure of the brain."[1]

Interestingly, this is the first discordant note in creation. Until this point, every time God creates He pronounces it good. The terminology of this first negative note expresses an incompleteness, a deficiency which God is now going to correct by creating a "helpmeet"—in Hebrew, quite literally a helper fit for him, one who is like himself, who corresponds to him—a spiritual partner who completes him.

What God does in preparation for creating Adam's helpmeet is fascinating. He has just declared that it's not good for Adam to be alone. But what does Adam know? He's walking around in the garden in delight, just happy to be there. No Fall yet, and he is enjoying everything with no clue what he's missing. So what does God do to clue him in?

> And out of the ground the LORD God formed
> every beast of the field, and every fowl of the air; and
> brought them unto Adam to see what he would call
> them: and whatsoever Adam called every living crea-
> ture, that was the name thereof. And Adam gave
> names to all cattle, and to the fowl of the air, and to
> every beast of the field; *but for Adam there was not
> found an help meet for him* [italics added].
> (Genesis 2:19–20 KJV)

God has all the creatures come by two by two. Along come a bull and a cow—the same, but different. Strutting up are a rooster and a hen—the same, but different. Now it's a stallion and a mare—the same, but different. This goes on and on and on. When it's all finished, Adam realizes there isn't someone like him, but different. Now that God has helped Adam understand that something's missing, even in paradise, He takes the next step in creation:

> And the LORD God caused a deep sleep to fall
> upon Adam, and he slept: and he took one of his ribs,
> and closed up the flesh instead thereof; And the rib,
> which the LORD God had taken from man, made
> he a woman, and brought her unto the man.
> (Genesis 2:21–22 KJV)

In Hebrew, the word translated "rib" literally means "a part of the side." It can refer to the side of a mountain, the side room of a house, a wing of the house, even a plank or supporting beam—all of these are usages in the Bible, and the principle is the same. The woman is formed from the man himself, making her of like nature: the same flesh, the same blood, equal in having the same faculties, and likewise in the image of God. By the physical mode of creation, Eve was inseparably connected to Adam.

God designed Adam for fulfillment through completion with his divinely given counterpart, in the divinely bestowed gift of marriage.

The origin of her creation ensured there could be absolute unity, a guarantee of the two becoming one flesh. And Adam said, "This *is* now bone of my bones, and flesh of my flesh: she shall be called Woman, because she was taken out of Man" (2:23 KJV). In verse 22 the word translated "made" is *banah* (pronounced "baw-naw") in Hebrew. It is more accurately translated "build." The woman is built to complete the creation of the human race, which began as a building in process but had not been complete until this final part was put into place, completing God's creation.

There are three and only three divinely ordained institutions in human society: the home, the church, and the government.

The Hebrew words for "male" and "female" in Genesis 1:27 are different from those for "man" and "woman" in Genesis 2:23. In the first passage, the male is *zakar* ("zaw-kawr") and the female is *naqebah* ("nek-ay-baw"), which have no kindred root, no similar sound, and are not of like appearance. In the second passage, when God is establishing man and woman as a unity, the woman is *'ishshah* ("ish-shaw"), and the man is *'isyh* ("eesh"), words that are alike in root and alike in sound, emphasizing that the two are made for each other.

LEAVING AND CLEAVING

It's worth learning Hebrew to read the literal translation of Genesis 2:23 because it is something like "Wow! That's it!" That's what was missing, says Adam, someone like me, but different! The next verse describes their unity: "Therefore shall a man leave his father and his mother, and shall cleave unto his wife; and they shall be one flesh. And they were both naked, the man and his wife, and were not ashamed" (Genesis 2:24 KJV).

We start off in life connected to our parents and honoring them as our primary family, but when we find God's intended life partner for us, we are to leave our father and our mother and cleave to our new partner. Failure to abide by this principle causes many, many difficulties and much marital discord—and it has fueled a popular television sitcom, *Everybody Loves Raymond*. This Emmy-award-winning show has struck a nerve with viewers in its humorous and poignant depictions of the ups and downs of marriage and family with parents/in-laws living right across the street. Ray's parents frequently drop in uninvited, and the tension between Ray's wife and Ray's meddling mother—every woman's mother-in-law nightmare—often leave Ray caught between pleasing one and disappointing the other.

I like to call this cleaving issue the "Mama, butt out!" principle. And let's be honest, it's mostly mamas doing the butting in, with only an occasional buttinsky dad. A husband's and a wife's primary loyalty and responsibility is to one another, but leaving mother and father and cleaving to your spouse is not quick and easy for most people.

Cleave is an interesting word. Back when Super Glue first appeared on the market I was insufficiently respectful of its properties, and I got my thumb and index finger stuck together with Super Glue. Now they were definitely attached; they had cleaved. There was no way I could get thumb and the finger apart without leaving some of the thumb on the finger and some of the finger on the thumb. It was a painful separation. That is exactly what happens when two people get married: they are Super Glued together, and that is why divorce is always so painful. It is the tearing apart of a cleaving together, and you leave part of yourself with the other person and they leave part of themselves with you.

SEX, LIES, AND THE BIBLE

God's design for union in marriage forms the basis of the essential and unique character of the sexual relationship. Keep the concept of cleaving in mind as you read Paul's admonition in 1 Corinthians 6:15–18, and notice that he quotes from Genesis 2:24 in this passage:

> Do you not know that your bodies are members of
> Christ himself? Shall I then take the members of
> Christ and unite them with a prostitute? Never!
> Do you not know that he who unites himself with a

prostitute is one with her in body? For it is said, "The two will become one flesh." But he who unites himself with the Lord is one with him in spirit.

Flee from sexual immorality. All other sins a man commits are outside his body, but he who sins sexually sins against his own body.

The word *flee* means to run, run, run. God created the sexual relationship for a purpose: to make of two people one person. Whether you intend it or not, whether you desire it or not, whether you want it or not, you cannot separate who you are from the sexual activities in which you engage. There is no such thing as merely casual or recreational sex.

Paul is saying nothing less profound than this: when you engage in sexual relations with a member of the opposite sex, you become part of that person and that person becomes part of you. A person who has not had sex is a different person than one who has—and, even more profoundly, a person who has been faithful to one marital partner is a different person than one who has been promiscuous with multiple sex partners, because every sexual encounter permanently leaves a part of each person in the other.

God's purpose for sex means that we cannot separate the intent from the action. This is a truth that desperately needs to be taught in our churches, especially to our young people. HBO and FOX certainly won't do it; neither will ABC and CBS and NBC. The public schools aren't going to do it. But the Bible says that parents are to rear their children in the knowledge and wisdom of the Lord, and we need to equip parents to speak in age-appropriate ways with their children about why God created them male and female. It's our responsibility and obligation. There has never been a time when it's been needed more, because the devil has decided to attack the Christian church in the beginning of the twenty-first century through sex. He is attempting to turn our nation into a sexually pagan country, and so far it looks like he is winning.

BREAKING UP IS TOO EASY TO DO

We also need to teach our young people and every member of the church that marriage is a divinely ordained institution. We ought to insist, absolutely, that churches require any couple who wants to get married to go through premarital counseling—and I don't mean a swipe here and a wave there. I mean premarital *counseling*: several sessions where it's made clear that they are making promises to God Almighty as well as to each other, and therefore "what God hath joined together let no man put asunder."

Would this work? It's already working at First Southern Baptist Church of Dell City, Oklahoma, one of our larger congregations, which has established a required premarital counseling program for anyone who wants to get married in their church. They reside in Oklahoma

County, which includes Oklahoma City, and that county has more divorces per capita than anywhere else in the country. Yet in eighteen years First Southern Baptist Church has seen only two couples get divorced. Later, both couples admitted to the church, "We told you what you wanted to hear at the time, but we were lying and we knew it." Their program flushes out engaged couples who discover they shouldn't get married by the time they finish the premarital counseling.

The devil has decided to attack the Christian church in the beginning of the twenty-first century through sex. ⌒

We also need to reinforce God's design for marriage by doing everything we can to support and undergird marriages that have already taken place. Older couples should be mentoring younger couples, helping them to understand the bumps in the road—which every marriage has. If you don't think your marriage has bumps in the road, you're either sleepwalking or in denial (and I don't mean the river in Egypt).

The sexual revolution has forced us to face some hard facts: a lot of what passed for biblical teaching about marriage and sex prior to the sexual revolution was sub-biblical. If you think God frowns on sex you need to read a good modern translation of the Song of Solomon.

Hebrews 13:4 declares the marriage bed undefiled and honorable in all. Sex isn't dirty; it's holy, and we need to treat it that way.

LOVE STORIES OF THE BIBLE

Sex within marriage is so holy that God uses the husband-wife relationship to describe His relationship with Israel in the Old Testament and Jesus' relationship with the church in the New Testament. Adam and Eve in the Garden is one of the two great biblical pictures of marriage. It is a wonderful story for a good marriage, speaking to our deepest longing for intimacy and completeness. Unless we have been granted the spiritual gift of celibacy (I have always felt that it's the easiest spiritual gift to discern whether you have it or not), God intends that the sense of incompleteness we are created with will impel us to seek our lifelong partner. As we grow into adulthood this longing intensifies, seeking its fulfillment in the intimacy of knowing and being known.

This holy longing is a prime target for the devil's perversion. In biblical understanding the sexual union of husband and wife is an act of giving themselves to each other, experiencing the deepest possible intimacy of knowing each other in love. What does the world do with this beautiful gift? It comes up with gutter terms for the sex act and makes them synonyms for acts of hostility, aggression, and exploitation. Parents today have a tough challenge of teaching their children the biblical understanding of human sexuality before they learn about it through the world's satanic counterfeit.

The lovely picture in the Garden of Eden didn't last, however. Adam and Eve fell in rebellion against God, which led to the second picture of love in the Bible. This is a picture for a hard marriage, and there are a lot of people today in hard marriages. This picture is a story of a faithful husband and his fickle wife, who leaves him and returns to him in cycles of bad times and good. It is the story of God and Israel, His recalcitrant bride who becomes an adulterous wife. But her lover does not suffer in silence. Like a tortured, hurting, betrayed husband who remonstrates with his faithless wife through the thin walls of an apartment, He pleads with her to return, to be faithful in her response to His love. She continues her adulterous ways, and He becomes righteously indignant with her, but He does not divorce her. He will not reject her. God never gives up, and ultimately His love will be requited when Israel finally accepts Him and the marriage becomes what God intended it to be at the Lamb's bridal supper.

THE HUSBAND, WIFE GOD WILL BLESS

We must do everything we can to build a fence of protection around marriage and teach what the Bible says about it. Husbands, you are to love your wives as Christ loved the church and gave Himself for it. What does that mean? Fortunately, we don't have to puzzle over it because we can simply read Paul's words to find out.

In the same way as Christ loved the church—an *agape* love—
"husbands ought to love their wives as their own bodies. He who
loves his wife loves himself. After all, no one ever hated his own
body, but he feeds and cares for it, just as Christ does the church—
for we are members of his body."

> *A* lot of what passed for
> biblical teaching about
> marriage and sex prior to
> the sexual revolution was
> sub-biblical.

This is the love Jesus describes in John 3:16: For God so *agaped*
the world that He gave His only begotten Son that whosoever believes
in Him should not perish but have life everlasting. That's an "in spite
of" kind of love, a love that endures all things. Paul wrote a Holy Spirit
inspired essay on *agape* that we have in 1 Corinthians chapter 13. This
is how a husband is to love his wife:

> Love is patient, love is kind. It does not envy, it
> does not boast, it is not proud. It is not rude, it is not
> self-seeking, it is not easily angered, it keeps no record
> of wrongs. Love does not delight in evil but rejoices
> with the truth. It always protects, always trusts, always
> hopes, always perseveres. (1 Corinthians 13:4–7)

There's no room in this description for a husband who thinks God has called him to be the dictator in his marriage. A husband who loves his wife as himself the way Christ loves the church is not going to say, "Woman, submit! The Bible says so." A husband who loves his wife the way Christ loves the church is going to bear all things, believe all things, hope all things, endure all things. His love will never fail. Do you know what that means? He isn't going to leave, period. He won't suffer in silence, but he will be kind and gentle, committed in sickness and health, in poverty and wealth, till death parts them.

Husbands are to love their wives; wives are to respect their husbands. This means to put yourself under the authority of your husband as unto the Lord (Ephesians 5:22). It's a reflection of her submission to God. It is not the husband's responsibility to make sure she does it; it's the wife's responsibility to do it voluntarily, without coercion.

When my wife and I conduct marriage retreats around the country, we use a questionnaire that asks both spouses to identify the top five things they most want and need from their spouse. And you know what's number one on the husband's list? Not sex—that's always in the top five, but it's not number one. Number one is, "I want my wife to respect me." How interesting that this is addressed in God's admonition to wives. Number one on the wife's list is, "I want my husband to be expressive and affectionate without an agenda for sex." Number two is help around the house. (Every time I read that I think about Dr. Laura saying that whenever she sees her husband vacuuming she considers it foreplay. I went home and asked my wife about the vacuum cleaner: "Where is that thing, and how do you use it?")

When Paul addressed the sexual struggles of the believers living in Corinth, he told them in 1 Corinthians chapter 7 that celibacy would be best, considering the debased culture that would make even New Orleans blush. However, Paul indicated, the power of the sexual impulse is such that to avoid immorality it would be better for them to marry:

> The husband should fulfill his marital duty to his
> wife, and likewise the wife to her husband. The wife's
> body does not belong to her alone but also to her
> husband. In the same way, the husband's body does
> not belong to him alone but also to his wife. Do not
> deprive each other except by mutual consent and for
> a time, so that you may devote yourselves to prayer.
> Then come together again so that Satan will not
> tempt you because of your lack of self-control. I say
> this as a concession, not as a command. I wish that
> all men were as I am. But each man has his own gift
> from God; one has this gift, another has that.
>
> Now to the unmarried and the widows I say: It is
> good for them to stay unmarried, as I am. But if they

cannot control themselves, they should marry, for it is better to marry than to burn with passion.
(1 Corinthians 7:3–9)

The word *deprive* is rendered "defraud" in the King James Version. It's a pretty strong word. When you do not meet your partner's sexual need, you are *defrauding* your mate. When you got married, you surrendered your right over your own body.

I was preaching on this at a town that shall remain nameless, and in the morning talk I said, "Maybe one of the best remedies for marriage problems is for us in the church to start a 'Just Say Yes' campaign." When I came back that evening to preach again, the chairman of the deacons and the minister of music were waiting for me on the front steps of the church.

"Rev. Land, we'd like to talk to you about that sermon you preached this morning."

"OK," I said.

"Well, we'd like to know if we could be the chairman and vice chairman of the 'Just Say Yes' campaign."

BECOMING THE FAMILY GOD WILL BLESS

It's no surprise that I have some profound policy disagreements with former Vice President Al Gore. But he said some very relevant, intelligent things when he spoke at his father's funeral: "My father, Albert

Gore, Sr., was the greatest man I ever knew." We should all aspire to earn our son's desire to say that about us. "And the greatest lesson that my father ever taught me," he said, "was the way he loved my mother. I knew that nothing was ever going to shatter my world." What did he mean by that? Quite simply this: he knew his dad was never going to leave his mother.

God intends that kind of security for every child. It's a telling difference that the biggest differences in lifestyle and personality between Al Gore and George W. Bush on the one hand, and Bill Clinton and Newt Gringrich on the other, can be traced to the fact that Al Gore and George W. Bush were raised in homes in which they knew their dad loved their mom and wouldn't leave, and Bill Clinton and Newt Gingrich didn't. Evidence continues to mount that divorce has devastating effects on children well into their adulthood.[2]

Sometimes God asks us uncomfortable questions. About twenty years ago while I was preparing to do a marriage retreat, God asked me such a question. It wasn't audible, and if anybody else had been there he probably wouldn't have heard it, but I sure did. God asked me, "Richard, are you the kind of husband you want your daughters to marry?"

I had never really thought about it like that. I mean I'm no perfect husband, that's for sure, but boy, I'm absolutely liberated compared to my dad. You know, my wife could have done a lot worse! But then I looked at myself and asked, *"Am I the kind of husband I want my*

THE FAMILY GOD WILL BLESS

daughters to marry?" I didn't like all the answers I got. My response to that question made me a better husband.

Well, dads, guess what? Every day, you are writing the description of your future son-in-law. Every day, in how you treat your wife, you are setting the standard for what your daughter will expect in a husband. How are you defining her future life partner? How do you like the answer?

Wives, are you the kind of wife you want your son to marry? Because every day, in the ways you behave toward your husband, you are setting the standard for what your son is going to expect in a wife. What kind of standard is it? How do you like the answer?

If we do not live by God's standard and salvage the divinely ordained institution of family, it will become an increasingly rare thing in our country, to the detriment of every child who has the misfortune to be born into a home that's going to be broken. Perhaps the greatest gift you can give your children—apart from telling them that Jesus loves them and Jesus died for them and Jesus has a wonderful plan for their lives—is to live before them what it means to be a godly husband or a godly wife. That's part of your calling in God's creation. Help your family to become one that God will bless.

10

The Church God Will Bless

I remember racing to get to the phone one time when I was about to do an interview. I was at home, barefoot, and the phone was in another part of the house. In my rush to get there, I dropped my briefcase on my big toe.

Never have I had such awareness of my big toe as I did at that moment.

I'd never really paid all that much attention to it, ever, until that incident. But even after the pain subsided and the toenail died and had to be removed, I'll tell you, my toe still had my attention.

Then an accident-prone friend of mine was mowing his lawn one day when he cut off more than the grass. He eventually recovered from the loss of his big toe, but he never recovered his balance while standing, walking, or running. The rest of his life he had to compensate for being without that relatively small part of his foot.

My soul, I have new respect for big toes.

In the church, some people are pinky fingers, others are hands, some stiffen the spine—but every member of the body of Christ is important. None of us can grow to what God wants us to be apart from ministering to others with our gifts and being ministered to by our fellow brothers and sisters who have been given gifts we don't have. Together, as Paul tells the Ephesians, we can grow in trying to plumb the depth and ascend the height and grasp the breadth of the love of our Lord and Savior Jesus Christ. We cannot grow to the stature of our Lord and Savior Jesus Christ alone. We are part of a body, and we have our spiritual gift not to enjoy by ourselves, but to minister to our brothers and sisters. The body is off balance if any part of it separates or cuts itself off from the rest.

> The church that God blesses
> is a gathering of people who
> love one another.

As one of three divinely ordained institutions, the church plays a central role in the life of the believer. Without the church, we cannot fulfill the biblical mandate for our families. Without the church, we would be scattered in our society like sheep without a shepherd, vulnerable to predators in the streets and in the corridors of power. What does the church God will bless look like?

A Gifted and Balanced Body

In a New Testament church, a local assembly is a baptized body of believers whose officers are pastors and deacons. It is the body of Christ, and the New Testament knows nothing of people who profess to be believers in the Lord Jesus Christ but are off alone doing their own thing.

God calls us to be in regular and consistent fellowship with our brothers and sisters in Christ in a local assembly of believers. Indeed, the Bible tells us not to forsake assembling ourselves together, as some do. Why is this so important? I think Paul answers this question for us in his first epistle to the Corinthians:

> Now about spiritual gifts, brothers, I do not want you to be ignorant. You know that when you were pagans, somehow or other you were influenced and led astray to mute idols. Therefore I tell you that no one who is speaking by the Spirit of God says, "Jesus be cursed," and no one can say, "Jesus is Lord," except by the Holy Spirit. There are different kinds of gifts, but the same Spirit. There are different kinds of service, but the same Lord. There are different kinds of working, but the same God works all of them in all men.

Now to each one the manifestation of the Spirit is
given for the common good. (1 Corinthians 12:1–7)

We know from this passage that everyone is given at least one spiritual
gift. And guess what? God decides what spiritual gifts you have; you
don't get to pick and choose, stamp your foot at God and say, "I want
this one!" You get the gift that God has given you.

God expects us to grow in our knowledge of Him and His Word. ⌐

My son, who is now in his mid-twenties, surrendered to the ministry, and who is attending Southeastern Baptist Theological Seminary
in Wake Forest, North Carolina, came to me a few years ago and said,
"Dad, I think God's calling me to preach."

"Well, son," I replied, "you know your mother and I have never
pushed you in that direction." But if genes in any way determine des-
tiny, it was predestined. I'm a deacon's kid. No pastors in my family,
but my wife, bless her heart, is the daughter, granddaughter, great-
granddaughter, niece, wife, and now mother of Baptist preachers.
That's a lot of chili powder in the chili, especially for someone who at
age fifteen was living in a parsonage in North Georgia during a particularly nasty church split and swore to her mother that the one thing

she would never do was marry a Baptist preacher. Now there are some who think she succeeded in that quest. Others would say the one thing you never want to do is tell God there's something you're not going to do, because that is what you will end up having to do.

"Son," I went on, "I'm convinced that when God calls you to preach He has ways of letting you know, and if you can stand to do something else then God didn't call you to preach. Because there are going to be days when the only thing that is going to sustain you is that you know God called you to do it." And that is the best reason for exercising your gift: because God gave it to you in order to edify the church:

> Now to each one the manifestation of the Spirit is
> given for the common good. To one there is given
> through the Spirit the message of wisdom, to another
> the message of knowledge by means of the same Spirit,
> to another faith by the same Spirit, to another gifts of
> healing by that one Spirit, to another miraculous pow-
> ers, to another prophecy, to another distinguishing
> between spirits, to another speaking in different kinds
> of tongues, and to still another the interpretation of
> tongues. All these are the work of one and the same
> Spirit, and he gives them to each one, just as he
> determines. (1 Corinthians 12:7–11)

God gives different gifts to different members of the body as He sees fit. I would encourage dear Pentecostal brethren to read this completely before insisting that the sign of being filled with the Spirit is speaking in tongues, because it says right here God gives these gifts to whomever He chooses to give them. Now by definition if it's still a valid gift, which remains a subject of disagreement in some circles, then it is something God gives to whomever He chooses and is not meant as universal for all the members of the body. Paul continues in chapter 12 to explain this principle of one body, many parts:

> The body is a unit, though it is made up of many
> parts; and though all its parts are many, they form one
> body. So it is with Christ. For we were all baptized by
> one Spirit into one body—whether Jews or Greeks,
> slave or free—and we were all given the one Spirit to
> drink.
>
> Now the body is not made up of one part but of
> many. If the foot should say, "Because I am not a
> hand, I do not belong to the body," it would not for
> that reason cease to be part of the body. And if the ear
> should say, "Because I am not an eye, I do not belong
> to the body," it would not for that reason cease to be
> part of the body. If the whole body were an eye, where
> would the sense of hearing be? If the whole body were
> an ear, where would the sense of smell be? But in fact

God has arranged the parts in the body, every one of
them, just as he wanted them to be. If they were all
one part, where would the body be? As it is, there are
many parts, but one body. (1 Corinthians 12:12–20)

At the moment of conversion, believers are baptized by the Holy
Spirit into the body of Christ. Water baptism is a symbol of that baptism by the Spirit that has already taken place. I sometimes wish Paul
would have added one more verse to this paragraph: "And if it were all
the tongue, where are the eyes?" It seems to me the surest sign of being
filled with the Spirit is not speaking in tongues, but getting control of
the one tongue we have.

A BODY ALIVE AND GROWING

A New Testament church performing in its proper sphere will first of
all be a church that is edifying its members and growing in Christ. Isn't
that what Paul says to the Corinthian church?

The man without the Spirit does not accept the
things that come from the Spirit of God, for they are
foolishness to him, and he cannot understand them,
because they are spiritually discerned. The spiritual man
makes judgments about all things, but he himself is not
subject to any man's judgment: "For who has known

the mind of the Lord that he may instruct him?" But

we have the mind of Christ. (1 Corinthians 2:14–16)

Dead men can't know about living things. The world is always going to think what we believe is foolishness because the Holy Spirit has not revealed to them that it is truth. Anytime persons are concerned about spiritual things or have an inkling that the Bible may be true, that is a sure sign that the Holy Spirit is convicting them. The natural man knows nothing about spiritual things. The spiritual man is the conqueror. The crybabies are the believers Paul addresses in chapter 3:

Brothers, I could not address you as spiritual but

as worldly—mere infants in Christ. I gave you milk,

not solid food, for you were not yet ready for it.

Indeed, you are still not ready. You are still

worldly. . . .

Paul's complaint against the Corinthian church was that there were a bunch of believers walking around with their spiritual umbilical cords looking for a place to plug them in. They never had the cord cut. Paul said it's all right to be a baby when you're a baby, but you Corinthian Christians are a case of spiritually arrested development. You are stalled in infancy; you have not been growing in grace.

God expects us to grow in our knowledge of Him and His Word. You don't have to be a rocket scientist to memorize a verse of Scripture each day in order to hide the Word of God in your heart that you might not sin against Him. A godly church equips its members by helping them identify, develop, and employ their ministry gifts for the edification of the body. That's absolutely essential, because it is part of the proclamation of the Word—both in word and in deed. A church that is growing in grace will not nullify in its actions the witness of the proclaimed Word from the pulpit.

SIGNS OF THE CHURCH GOD BLESSES

Hebrews chapter 13 provides a wonderful picture of what the church that God will bless looks like. Here are eight signs of churches that understand their proper sphere and actively engage in their God-ordained ministry in the world.[1]

(1) They love one another. Hebrews 13:1 exhorts, "Keep on loving each other as brothers." A church that God blesses is a gathering of people who love one another.

It's a disgrace that too often we Baptists are known by our backbiting and infighting. They say that where there are two Baptists there are at least three opinions. What did they say in the first century about the Christians? Behold these Christians, the Book of Acts tells us, how they love one another. Now, I didn't say that we liked one another.

Think about your extended family. Do you like everybody in your extended family? I doubt it. But you love them, right? They're kin. Blood's thicker than water. I don't have much in common with some of my extended family, but if they were ever in trouble I'd be the first one there to help them, and they'd be the first ones here to help me, because we're blood.

Christians are blood brothers and sisters with a common Father. We have entered into a new family. I can remember going to a football game just a few weeks after a mission trip to Russia. I was in my hometown of Houston, Texas, preached on Sunday morning and on Sunday afternoon went to see the Oakland Raiders play the then Houston Oilers, in the days before they defected to Tennessee as the Titans. I grew up close to the Astrodome, so this was all part of home for me. But that day I was seated in the middle of the biggest bunch of loud-mouth drunks I'd ever seen at a sports event, or anywhere else for that matter. It practically made me ashamed to be an American.

At that game I thought about how three weeks before I had been in Russia, our former enemy, just a month after the Soviet Union ceased to exist. I was with so many Baptists who wanted to worship in this little church building that they were holding six services on Sunday, and people were still standing outside in the snow with the windows open so they could hear the sermon. (We all had communion with a common cup, and I don't think I've ever experienced such hygienic intimacy with so many people.) I was acutely aware that I had been more at home with my Russian brothers and sisters in Christ in the nation of our former sworn enemy than I was sitting in a football stadium about fifteen blocks from the house where I grew up with people who did not know Jesus as Savior and Lord.

(2) They practice hospitality. Hebrews 13:2 admonishes us, "Do not forget to entertain strangers, for by so doing some people have entertained angels without knowing it." The church that God blesses is a hospitable church. It's a friendly church. The Southern Baptist Convention conducted some studies about why people join churches, and it really wounded the egos of our preachers. The preaching was fifth or sixth on the list. The first three things were variations on, "They made me feel welcome. They acted like they cared about me. They made me feel at home, as if they wanted me to be there." And I hate to give worship leaders this kind of power, but the fourth reason was music—before the preaching. Amazing, isn't it?

"*Noncontroversial Gospel*"
is an oxymoron.

The church God uses is a warm and welcoming place where people feel wanted. A church in which most people do not feel welcome is not in God's will. Who else should be welcoming sinners than the church?

(3) They have a compassionate heart. "Remember those in prison as if you were their fellow prisoners, and those who are mistreated as if you yourselves were suffering" (Hebrews 13:3). A godly church has a compassionate heart. It is not insensitive to suffering. It is willing to suffer with those who suffer as though they were in bonds with them, and they will do something about it. They will go out and be salt and light.

(4) They are sexually pure. Hebrews 13:4 declares, "Marriage should be honored by all, and the marriage bed kept pure, for God will judge the adulterer and all the sexually immoral." The church God blesses is a pure church. Everyone is welcome, but not everyone welcome is a member in good standing. In our age of pagan sexuality, we seem to have forgotten to defend the purity of the bride of Christ. We need to speak the truth in love—what is sometimes called "tough love"—in confronting our brothers and sisters in Christ who are bringing reproach and embarrassment to the Gospel of Christ by their behavior. Better for us to do it than for the Lord to have to do it, because He has all kinds of ways of getting people's attention.

Years ago I had a friend in the ministry who was heading for shipwreck, plain as the nose on your face. I took him to lunch and said, "Brother, I don't want to hurt your feelings, but I want to ask you a question. Have you lost your mind?"

"What do you mean?"

When I told him my concerns he protested, "There isn't anything going on between us."

"Oh please," I said. "Please. There may not be anything yet, but you're thinking about it and so is she!"

"I can't believe you're saying that," he retorted.

"Oh please," I said, "come *on* now."

We parted over lunch without resolution, but later on he came back to me and said, "I want to thank you. I was so mad at you I could have hit you, but I want to thank you because you were right. My wife and I were going through a rocky patch and my secretary was *sympathetic*."

That's why I have a rule. I'm not saying anyone else has to follow it, but it's my rule: I'm not alone with any woman other than my mom, my wife, or my daughters, period. I tell people when I go somewhere that if a woman is coming to pick me up at the airport, please make certain a second person joins her, because I will not get into a car with a woman alone, period. And I don't have breakfast, lunch, or dinner with a woman other than my wife or my mom or my daughters unless there are other folks at the table. I'm just not going to do it.

> *Jesus has commanded us to be a moral disinfectant in the world.*

(5) They are concerned with treasures in heaven, not on earth. The fifth sign of the church that God blesses is in verse 5: "Keep your lives free from the love of money and be content with what you have, because God has said, 'Never will I leave you; never will I forsake you.'" A church that is more concerned with how much money it has in the bank than how many people it's winning to the Lord is not a church God's going to use, because it's laying up treasures on earth instead of in heaven. Yes, it's critical that churches are financially responsible, but there are too many that are preoccupied with material gains instead of using the talents and the financial resources God has given them to reach the world for the Lord Jesus Christ.

(6) They have godly pastoral authority. "Remember your leaders, who spoke the word of God to you," Hebrews 13:7 instructs. "Consider the outcome of their way of life and imitate their faith." When God calls a man to preach, He also gives him the gift of teaching. Paul spells this out in 1 Timothy chapter 3. Deacons only receive and hold sound doctrine; the pastor has to teach sound doctrine.

God calls us to be in regular
and consistent fellowship with
our brothers and sisters in
Christ in a local assembly
of believers.

The writer to the Hebrews instructs believers later in chapter 13, "Obey your leaders and submit to their authority. They keep watch over you as men who must give an account. Obey them so that their work will be a joy, not a burden, for that would be of no advantage to you" (v. 17). The pastoral office is a position of authority. There are no great committee-led churches; there are no great deacon-led churches. There are only great pastor-led and deacon-supported churches. The language here is the same phrase Paul uses in Ephesians when he instructs wives to submit to their husbands. It's not the pastor's job to tell the people to submit. It's the people's job to put themselves under the authority of their pastor. Because he has an awesome job, to give an account of his watchcare of the people's souls.

The church that God blesses understands and practices pastoral authority. Churches need to understand that when they call a man to be their pastor, they're not saying they like the way his wife plays the piano. They're not saying, "He fits our age parameter and profile—age forty with thirty years' experience." They're saying, "We believe this is God's man to be our shepherd, and we're going to follow him unless in conscience we cannot."

Does this mean the pastor is a dictator? No, of course not. There's a very interesting parallel in how God instructs husbands: "love your wives the way Christ loved the church." That's servant love: he is to submit himself to his wife by giving himself to her and loving her sac-rificially. He will always put her needs above his own—not above the Lord's, but above his own. God instructs wives to put themselves under their husband's authority as unto the Lord. God instructs the people to submit themselves to the authority of those in leadership. But when God instructs the pastors in 1 Peter 5:1–4, He is very specific about how they are to exercise authority:

> To the elders among you, I appeal as a fellow elder, a witness of Christ's sufferings and one who also will share in the glory to be revealed. Be shepherds of God's flock that is under your care, serving as overseers—not because you must, but because you are willing, as God wants you to be; not greedy for money, but eager to serve; not lording it over those entrusted to you, but being examples to the flock. And when the Chief Shepherd appears, you will receive the crown of glory that will never fade away.

This is one of the most important passages in the New Testament concerning the pastoral office, because it uses all three descriptive terms depicting the pastor's role. "Elders," or *presbuteros* ("pres-boo-ter-os"), is a generic term for a mature man. The respect due to such a man is transferred to the office of pastor.

The second descriptive term is the phrase "Be shepherds," also translated "Feed," from the Greek *poimaino* ("poy-mah-ee-no")—to feed a flock of sheep, to shepherd, to provide pasture. The pastor is to be a shepherd who knows and loves the sheep, who understands his role as protector of the sheep. This is what the Lord said to Peter— "Do you love me? Then feed my sheep" (see John 21:15–18).

Serving as *overseers,* or taking the *oversight,* is the third word, translated from the Greek *episkopountes,* "to oversee"; the noun form is *episkopos,* the overseer. This is often rendered "bishop," meaning a pastor who superintends in a position of authority—those to whom Hebrews 13:17 instructs the people to submit. But God tells the preachers not to lord it over the flock.

A godly church equips its members by helping them identify, develop, and employ their ministry gifts for the edification of the body.

In his book *The Reformed Pastor,* the great seventeenth-centuryr Puritan preacher Richard Baxter criticized those pastors who try to make their sermons difficult for the people to understand so that the people will understand the pastor knows more than they do. Baxter is right to condemn such a pastoral posture, because it's a contradiction of this passage in 1 Peter.[2] You don't lord it over the flock, you give your life in service to the flock. In marriage, problems arise when the husband does not take responsibility or the wife rebels against it. This is also true in the church. Problems arise with pastors who won't lead and people who won't follow godly leadership.

I have found that people are desperate for preachers with a backbone who will stand up and lead. The best of God's people don't rebel against this kind of authority; they welcome it. "Finally," they say, "we've found a preacher who isn't mealymouthed and afraid he's going to offend somebody, somewhere, sometime. He will cut straight to the point and tell it like it is." People will take a lot from you if they know you love them and you are protective of them as you seek to build them up in the faith.

(7) **They preach and practice sound doctrine.** The seventh sign of the church God uses is that it preaches, practices, and proclaims sound doctrine:

> Jesus Christ is the same yesterday and today and
> forever.
> Do not be carried away by all kinds of strange
> teachings. It is good for our hearts to be strengthened
> by grace, not by ceremonial foods, which are of no
> value to those who eat them. (Hebrews 13:8–9)

I love what Methodist theologian Thomas Oden said about theology as he wrote eloquently of his journey into neoapostasy and back to orthodoxy. He said from the first moment he thought of becoming a theologian he was urged "to 'think creatively' and to make 'some new contribution' to theology." After many years of study and much hard-won wisdom he now had a new and very different vision:

I once had a curious dream that rekindled my
deepest theological hopes. The only scene I can
remember was in the New Haven cemetery, where
I accidentally stumbled over my own tombstone only
to be confronted by this astonishing epitaph: "He
made no new contribution to theology." I was mar-
velously pleased by the idea and deeply assured. Why?
Because I have of late been trying in my own way to
follow the mandate of Irenaeus "not to invent new
doctrine." No concept was more deplored by the early
ecumenical councils than the notion that theology's
task was to "innovate" (*neo-terizein*), which to them
implied some imagined creative addition to the apos-
tolic teaching. . . .[3]

The church that God blesses understands that we serve a changeless
Christ who will meet all the needs of an ever-changing world. It takes
all of its experience to the Lord for testing. If experience conflicts with
the Bible's teaching they will reject experience, not the Word of God.

(8) They proclaim the Gospel in word and deed. The eighth
and final sign of the church God will bless is found in Hebrews
13:15: "Through Jesus, therefore, let us continually offer to God
a sacrifice of praise—the fruit of lips that confess his name." The
church on God's mission proclaims the Gospel, witnesses to
the Gospel, is always ready to give a reasonable explanation of

the hope that lies within it, and does not forget to do good works. If we're going to be godly men and women in that church, we will heed the command of our Lord and Savior Jesus Christ to be the salt of the earth and the light of the world.

I'm very thankful for my Southern Baptist heritage. I'm grateful that I was reared in a home in which it was taught that Jesus loves us, died for us, and has a wonderful plan for our lives if we confess our sin and trust Him as Savior and Lord. I'm grateful that I was reared in Southern Baptist churches which always emphasized that salvation is by grace alone through faith, there is nothing we can do to earn salvation, and Christianity is first and last a personal relationship with Jesus Christ as *our* Lord, not just *the* Lord.

> People are desperate for preaches with backbone who will stand up and lead.

But there's one thing I heard growing up in those Southern Baptist churches on the Gulf Coast of Texas that was just plain wrong. It usually went something like this: "Because we're Southern Baptists, we don't get involved in anything controversial. We just preach the Gospel." That's an oxymoron. As a graduate of Oxford I hasten to add that an oxymoron is not a moron who went to Oxford. It's a figure of speech describing something in mutually contradictory terms—such as, for instance, "humble Texan." Trust me: that is an oxymoron.

"Noncontroversial Gospel" is an oxymoron. There is something in the Gospel to offend all fallen flesh, sooner or later. Paul confirmed that all who live a godly life in Christ will suffer. Jesus told us we would suffer, right before He commanded us to be salt and light:

> Blessed are you when people insult you, persecute
> you and falsely say all kinds of evil against you because
> of me. Rejoice and be glad, because great is your
> reward in heaven, for in the same way they persecuted
> the prophets who were before you. (Matthew 5:11–12)

Immediately following this declaration, He gives us our ministry mandate:

> You are the salt of the earth. But if the salt loses its
> saltiness, how can it be made salty again? It is no
> longer good for anything, except to be thrown out and
> trampled by men. You are the light of the world. A city
> on a hill cannot be hidden. Neither do people light a
> lamp and put it under a bowl. Instead they put it on
> its stand, and it gives light to everyone in the house. In
> the same way, let your light shine before men, that
> they may see your good deeds and praise your Father
> in heaven. (Matthew 5:13–16)

Why this juxtaposition? Because salt is a preservative against decay, but in order to preserve and purify it needs to come into contact with what needs preserving. If we're going to obey this command, there's no place for withdrawing from the world and saying we're not going to get involved. Salt is a purifying agent to keep dead things from rotting.

But what else does salt do? It burns, stings, and irritates. This is what will happen if we are obedient in refusing to hide our light under a bushel, instead allowing it to shine so that nonbelievers will see our good works and exclaim, "There really is a God! He must be worthy of praise!" Light gives life, penetrating darkness and dispelling gloom, but that light will provoke opposition. The Bible tells us that people love darkness rather than light because darkness hides their evil deeds. You go shining light into dark places and people are going to start taking shots at your headlights.

Jesus has commanded us to be a moral disinfectant in the world. This means we have an obligation in our sphere of influence as the church to be out there in society as salt and light. This means not simply opposing abortion, but proclaiming that every life is valuable to God. In the same breath that the writer to the Hebrews exhorts us to praise, he also prompts us to remember to do good works. The idea that there are two Gospels, a social one and a spiritual one, was hatched in the pits of hell. There's only one Gospel, and it's a whole Gospel for whole people.

Don't get me wrong: it isn't blasphemous for Christians to go out into the world and feed the hungry without telling them about the bread of life; to house the homeless without telling them that in our Father's house are many mansions; to clothe the naked without teaching them to put on the whole armor of God. However, it is a denial of our Savior's incarnation to proclaim the Gospel while remaining blind to the fact that people are hungry, thirsty, naked, and homeless. God calls us to both in the ministry of the whole Gospel.

> The idea that there are two Gospels, a social one and a spiritual one, was hatched in the pits of hell. There's only one Gospel, and it's the whole Gospel for whole people.

If we are the people God blesses, if we are the spouses, parents, and families God blesses, then we will be members of churches God blesses, and we will be fulfilling God's plan for us to be the salt of the earth and the light of the world. We will be reaching out to those in need. We will be known as compassionate, caring people—hospitable and friendly. We will step out into the culture seeking to preserve it against decay, to stop the rot, to inoculate against moral and spiritual infection. We will not be huddling together in private communions of the saints. It means we will be active in a community filled with such churches, giving themselves in service to the Lord, to one another, and to the world.

God has given us an awesome privilege and responsibility to be members of the body of Christ. Do you know what your gifts are? Are you letting God hone those gifts? Are you sharing them with your brothers and sisters in Christ? Are you teaching your people what God's Word says about the responsibilities of the people and their pastors? May God make each of us what He wants us to be.

II

THE COMMUNITY GOD WILL BLESS

"Moral reform is a frustrating and ultimately impossible task," warns a leading voice calling Christians away from social and political involvement to concentrate only on proclaiming the Gospel.[1] Consider this statement next to the efforts of Bob Macy, the district attorney for Oklahoma County, who prevailed in wielding the law to shut down businesses involved in sexually explicit, pornographic materials. During a period between 1983 and 1989, while the incidence of rape statewide increased 22 percent, it decreased 27 percent in Oklahoma County. That means that 1,916 women and girls were saved from this brutal crime.

Frustrating and ultimately impossible?

The terrible evil of slavery survived two great spiritual awakenings in America. Christians who were proclaiming salvation in Jesus Christ were among those who tacitly or explicitly endorsed it. Abraham Lincoln devoted nearly sixteen years of public service fighting against it, on Christian grounds, until he succeeded in passing the Thirteenth Amendment to the Constitution in 1865. Several years later, the passage of the Fifteenth Amendment ensured that no American citizen would be denied voting rights based on race.

While proclamation-only advocates denounce "political movements and moral crusades," they do affirm the rightness of Christians opposing "the sins of our society, and it is right that Christians as individuals should voice our objection in the voting booth and by speaking out in other ways."[2] Yet African-Americans seeking to vote their Christian conscience were denied that right for nearly one hundred years after the abolition of slavery until the Voting Rights Act of 1965. How would evangelism-only Christians respond today if some states denied evangelical Christians their right to vote because of their religious convictions? Would they continue to shun political involvement and focus only on winning souls, not voting rights?

> *A* community under the sway of the Gospel holds up righteous and holy models to young people.

Legalized racial segregation flourished during most of the twentieth century in the Bible-belt South, demographically the most heavily-concentrated population of self-identified Christians of any region in the country. Without the moral crusade of Martin Luther King, Jr., and other Christian leaders, the Civil Rights Movement would not have happened as it did, and segregation might be flourishing still.

Political involvement and moral campaigns: frustrating and ultimately impossible in changing the leopard's spots? Not for slaves. Not for African-Americans seeking basic rights of citizenship. Not for the women and girls of Oklahoma County.

Perhaps the command for Christians to be salt and light includes seeking to make our communities places where children and women are safe, where people of different races are treated with equal rights and respect, where inhabitants are not exposed on every street corner to immorality, where every human life is valued, where it is easier to do and say the right thing and harder to do and say the wrong thing.

HEALING AMERICA: REFORM OR REVIVAL?

As our communities continue to suffer from the accelerating moral disintegration of our society at large, people of religious faith turn to their religious convictions seeking answers to the moral and spiritual malaise that afflicts us. They face criticism from two sides: pietists who criticize Christians for getting involved with political reform, and secularists who assert that church-state separation requires Christian involvement to be eliminated from the public square.

It is critical for our country that Christians understand that both criticisms are wrong. Clearly, attempts to rectify societal immorality and injustice by political and governmental reform alone are doomed to failure. However, the premise that Christians should focus *only* on evangelism is just as wrong as the premise that political reform *alone* is sufficient. Christians have a responsibility to do both if we are to help shape communities that God will bless.

> The salt of the law can change actions, but only the light of the Gospel can change attitudes.

We have already looked at several positive examples of reform. However, it is futile to attempt change through reform alone, ignoring the need to change hearts through evangelism and discipleship. King Josiah stands as the classic example that governmental reform alone is never enough (see 2 Kings chapters 22 and 23). After Josiah's heart was changed by the Word of God, he carried out a thorough reform of the nation, rooting out idolatrous and wicked behavior. Sadly, this change proved to be cosmetic, because only the people's habits were changed, not their hearts. When the king died, all of his reforms died with him.

But we could have a great revival in America and still be oppressed by evil unless everyone in America were saved, which the Bible tells us is not going to happen. The road to perdition is wide, and the gate of salvation is narrow. Even if 30 or 40 percent of the population were genuine born-again believers, taking a stand against evil, there would still be a percentage of the population who would say, "Sure, you're entitled to your opinion. But if I want to beat my wife, I'll do it. You're entitled to your opinion, but if I want to torture my animals, I'll do it. You're entitled to your opinion, but if I want to beat up on black people and homosexuals, I'll do it." That's why God ordained civil government. Revival alone isn't enough, and "moralism" alone isn't enough. We need both, and that starts with Christians getting right with God.

But it doesn't end with God's people getting right with God. God's people have got to go out and behave like God's people. If we refuse to use God's divinely ordained magistrate, civil government, by saying, "No, you can't kill your unborn baby or your just-born baby; no, you can't euthanize your elderly and sick grandmother," and we allow those evils to persist, God will judge us instead of bless us.

God will not bless us if we permit gross immorality and gross injustice to go unchecked in our society. During the slavery era, a significant portion of the South was arguably full of born-again Christians. God allowed cataclysmic judgment to come upon that civilization in the form of the Civil War, because they allowed and supported human bondage.

SALT OF THE LAW, LIGHT OF THE GOSPEL

The culture can be seasoned with the salt of the law, because the law can change actions. Because the South used to be the most segregated part of the country, the civil rights laws applied in the thirteen states where there were systemic patterns of racial segregation in a way they didn't apply in California, Colorado, or Oregon. The Southern states were held to stricter legal standards than the rest of the country. And guess what? In thirty years, the South went from being the most segregated part of the country to being the most integrated part of the country.

I don't favor Prohibition, but there is evidence that when it took effect, a great number of people quit drinking simply because it was illegal. The law does have power, but it has limitations, and it needs to be coupled with the light of the Gospel:

- The salt of the law can change actions, but only the light of the Gospel can change attitudes.
- The salt of the law can change behaviors, but only the light of the Gospel can change beliefs.
- The salt of the law can change habits, but only the light of the Gospel can change hearts.

As Christians, we are called to implement the salt of the law and shine the light of the Gospel. We have a responsibility to teach

Christians that it's wrong to kill their babies, and we have a responsibility to prevent non-Christian people from killing their babies. We have a responsibility to teach Christians that it's wrong to be prejudiced against people of other ethnic groups, and we have a responsibility to prevent prejudiced non-Christians—and carnal Christians—from denying people of other ethnic groups their basic constitutional rights.

> *God's people have got to go out and behave like God's people.*

The withdrawal of evangelicals from social and political engagement for too many years has led to many of our nation's problems. We must never embrace the false dichotomy of reform *or* revival, but reform *and* revival simultaneously. And when that happens, an exciting equation emerges: "revival + reform = reformation." And reformation is what our communities and our nation desperately need. Nothing less is required, and nothing else will suffice.

BLIND SPOTS IN CHRISTIAN VISION

As we've seen, conversion doesn't simply eliminate the blind spots we inherit from our culture. The two classic examples from former eras in which far higher percentages of the population were Christian are race and gender.

But there is a third Christian blind spot we haven't yet discussed: the lack of a proper understanding of our responsibility in the compassionate use of wealth. In the late nineteenth century, there was too much acceptance of social Darwinism in the Christian faith; as a result, many thought, *We are wealthy and rich because we are the fittest . . . our wealth means that God is rewarding our achievements . . . poverty is a sign of our own weakness, sloth, or moral inferiority . . .* and so forth.

> The salt of the law can change behaviors, but only the light of the Gospel can change beliefs.

In actual fact, there were a lot of forces at play over which individuals had no choice. The changes brought on by industrialization could have been carried out far more compassionately than they were, but there was no safety net for the working classes and no real understanding of the cultural, economic, and social forces involved.

The Gospel has responsibilities that begin with spiritual commitments, but spiritual commitments involve obligations to others—not just saved people, but lost people, and not just lost souls, but souls and bodies that are being victimized. That's why Hebrews 13 is careful to include the commands to be compassionate and hospitable. Repenting, praying, and seeking God must begin with people being converted, but the converted have a responsibility to go out into society. They have an obligation to the unconverted, which goes beyond witnessing to them, into all spheres of life—because we have a Gospel that penetrates and changes all spheres of life.

SIGNS OF A COMMUNITY GOD WILL BLESS

A society that God blesses is under the sway of the Gospel of Jesus Christ. What would be the chief signs of healing in our society if enough Christians were laying hold of God's 2 Chronicles 7:14 promise individually, in their families, and in their churches?

I think the first change we would notice is a strong societal tilt against pagan sexuality.

We would also see a strong societal tilt against pagan assaults on the sanctity of life in all its forms. A healing community would stand against pagan human sacrifices of unborn children, of the elderly and infirm, of the mentally retarded.

A community under God's blessing instead of God's judgment would tilt toward a more magnanimous use of wealth by individuals and by groups. I'm not talking about coerced redistribution, but far more generous giving and compassionate use of wealth by believers and churches.

An America of healing communities would be a land far less wracked by prejudice, far less degraded by sexual immorality, far less damaged by the horrific effects of sexual immorality. It would be a land less fractured in its most intimate places of marriages and families. It would not have over 50 percent of its children growing up in broken homes and 45 percent of children fatherless after age six. Its communities would be shaped by a significant portion of the population seeking to embrace God's understanding of marriage and practicing God's intentions for sexuality and following God's instructions for familial responsibilities.

Withdrawal of evangelicals from social and political engagement for too many years has led to many of our nation's problems.

These social values would be reflected in the law. Legal codes would support and strengthen marriage while penalizing divorce. There would be far more severe penalties for child desertion, because children would be revalued in this society. In fifty years we've changed from a child-centered society to a child-neglecting society, a child-abusing society, a child-killing society, a society that more often views children as burdens rather than blessings. That dark development would reverse itself. A nation under God's healing would welcome *all* children, whether they met some human arbitrary standards of normalcy or not.

Communities of blessing would define and identify deviant behavior, tolerating it only in private between consenting adults if no compelling public health reasons required its legal restriction. Affirming marriage would mean denouncing adultery as sin, not just another lifestyle choice. It would mean define homosexuality and lesbianism as deviant and unhealthy, not just another lifestyle choice. But there would still be a price to pay in public, because it would not be celebrated as healthy and commendable. It shouldn't be my business unless they make it my business by asserting it publicly, and then it becomes the public's business.

A community under the sway of the Gospel would hold up righteous and holy models to young people, not celebrities who spend their fabulous wealth on self-indulgent, immoral lifestyles or pop icons who parade their personal deviancy as entertainment or leaders who lie to cover up their sin and then slice and dice morality down to what the meaning of *is* is. A healing community will elect righteous men and women to serve in public office, and then we will have the kind of government God will bless.

WHAT IF THE END IS NEAR?

There is a disturbing tendency among Christians today to shrug off the mandates of the Gospel in our culture and to withdraw to Christian ghettoes because they presume the return of Christ is imminent. If the world is just going to get worse and worse until the Lord comes, why should we be involved as salt and light? And why should we be trying to make America a nation God would bless when it's just not realistic to believe it could ever recover from the depths to which it has sunk?

The salt of the law can change habits, but only the light of the Gospel can change hearts.

Just for the record, I would state my own position as a pretribulation premillennalist. Perhaps I should call this the optimistic premillennalist view, because I believe the church is going to be raptured before the tribulation. I take the Book of Revelation as it was intended to be taken, as a literal and apocalyptic book. I believe that from chapter 4, verse 1 through the end of the book, Revelation prophesies events that are triggered by the snatching away of the church, commencing the tribulation period of seven years, which is then followed by the cataclysmic events at the end of that period, leading to the millennial reign and culminating in the new heaven and new earth. In other words, Tim LaHaye and I have little if any disagreement about eschatology.

However, the Bible tells us that no one knows the hour or the day of Christ's coming, and we're not the first ones in the history of the church to think we're living in the end times. In the first half of the twentieth century, many Christians thought Italian dictator Mussolini was the Antichrist. After all, he was trying to revive the Roman Empire in Rome. Many others thought Hitler was the Antichrist—he was a pretty good imitation, and he certainly provided plenty of justification.

There have been many epochs in history leading Christians to read signs of the end times, but the reality is only God knows the hour or the day of His coming. And there is nothing in the Bible that would preclude another great revival before Jesus comes back. "If my people" experienced a great repentance from sin and a deep longing for God's blessing, it could lead to a great spiritual awakening, even to a reformation—a society as transformed by God's people as Europe was rocked by Calvin and Luther, as England was galvanized by Whitfield and Wesley, as colonial America was electrified by Edwards. This reformation might change the direction of our nation as did the great revivals of 1858 and the sweeping social changes to pre-Civil War America. We just don't know what God might be gracious to accomplish through us, prior to the final descent into apostasy and moral and spiritual degradation triggering the events of the tribulation and the horrendous fulfillment of the prophecies of the Book of Revelation.

God has not called us to be seers or prophets; He has called us to be obedient. And we know that if we are obedient, we will invoke His blessings. We know that it is His will for all of us to be His people. It is His desire for every individual to be saved and come to a full knowledge of the truth. God is not willing that any should perish.

I'm not a Calvinist, so I believe in God's Gospel for everyone. I believe that if we are obedient, then God's blessings will come. And if enough of us become Christians and are obedient, if enough of us live like the disciples God has called us to be, then God's blessings will come according to God's spiritual calendar. However the timing of the blessing, the moment when the divine critical mass is reached, is up to God, not us.

> If enough of us live like the disciples God has called us to be, then God's blessings will come according to God's spiritual calendar.

If we seek to know the law of the Lord and do it, and teach its statutes and judgments as did Ezra, then we will know what it means to be God's man or God's woman, in God's place in God's time, on God's business with God's blessing. If enough of us do this, we have God's promise that He will pour down blessings on America.

12

THE GOVERNMENT GOD WILL BLESS

What does a government ordained by God look like? For the apostle Paul writing to the Romans, it was the Roman Empire—not what you would call an enlightened regime. You and I wouldn't like it even if we were Roman citizens. Yet Paul referred to these pagan rulers as governing authorities established by God, and he instructed persecuted Christians to submit to them:

> Everyone must submit himself to the governing
> authorities, for there is no authority except that which
> God has established. The authorities that exist have
> been established by God. Consequently, he who rebels
> against the authority is rebelling against what God has
> instituted, and those who do so will bring judgment
> on themselves. (Romans 13:1–2)

Americans are fortunate to have a much higher standard of government: of the people, by the people, and for the people, founded on the principle that all people are endowed by their Creator with certain unalienable rights. Don't ever let anybody tell you that the founding document of the United States is the Constitution. The Constitution is really the enabling document for the founding document of our nation, the Declaration of Independence.

Government, along with its appointed officials, is ordained by God to curtail evil in the world. That is its primary responsibility: to protect those who do right and punish those who do wrong.

> For rulers hold no terror for those who do right,
> but for those who do wrong. Do you want to be free
> from fear of the one in authority? Then do what is
> right and he will commend you. For he is God's ser-
> vant to do you good. But if you do wrong, be afraid,
> for he does not bear the sword for nothing. He is
> God's servant, an agent of wrath to bring punish-
> ment on the wrongdoer. (Romans 13:3–4)

Our Christian obligation is to support the government through tribute and through taxation. It is our godly duty to obey the law even when no one's looking: "Therefore it is necessary to submit to the authorities, not only because of possible punishment, but also because of conscience" (Romans 13:5). It is our godly duty to obey the laws even if we disagree with them, unless in doing so we would disobey God, and seek to change them in a peaceful manner. We are to render unto Caesar the things that are Caesar's and unto God the things that are God's.

In February 2001 the government conducted a peaceful raid to confiscate the property of Indianapolis Baptist Temple and turn it over to the IRS after the church refused to pay withholding taxes from its payroll for nearly two decades, claiming that it could not be regulated by the federal government and that church workers were responsible for paying all their taxes on their own. This church was disobeying Paul's command in Romans 13:6–7: "This is also why you pay taxes, for the authorities are God's servants, who give their full time to governing. Give everyone what you owe him: If you owe taxes, pay taxes; if revenue, then revenue; if respect, then respect; if honor, then honor."

We need to obey the law and pay our taxes. If we don't, we can expect that sooner or later the hammer of the government will come down and we will have brought reproach upon the Gospel.

We have a ministry to the world as salt and the light, and we all have responsibilities to the civil authorities. A biblical lifestyle requires us to maintain the proper balance between the three divinely ordained institutions of family, church, and government. The Indianapolis congregation had clearly allowed their sphere of church to lean so far over on the government sphere that in this instance, it obliterated their duty to the government. Did they experience God's judgment? It certainly wasn't blessing.

SORTING OUT CHURCH-STATE CONFUSION

The separation of church and state is one of the most misunderstood, misconstrued, and misapplied concepts in our society. The mistake that most people make is assuming there are only two options: government *acknowledgment* of religion or government *avoidance* of religion. Both are flawed models that will not maximize religious freedom in a democratic society. Our best model is a secular state that *accommodates* the people's right to express their own religious views according to the dictates of their own consciences.

As an example, let's consider the issue of displaying a manger scene on the courthouse lawn. The avoidance position contends that the government should banish nativity scenes on the courthouse lawn (or posting of the Ten Commandments in public places) because any display on government property constitutes an endorsement, and thus a violation of the separation of church and state. The acknowledgment position would argue for tax-funded religious displays on government property according to the nation's majority religion.

A third position, which I believe to be the most biblical position, is *accommodation,* which contends that the government should accommodate the rights of individuals of any religion to express their religious beliefs in public locales. Therefore, the government would be overstepping its authority to deny people the right to put a manger scene on the public's courthouse lawn. If a group of Christian citizens wants to buy a manger scene and display it on the lawn during the Christmas season, if the Jewish community wants to provide a Jewish symbol during Hanukkah, if Muslims want to install a display honoring Ramadan, then the government should accommodate the people's right to express their convictions in that way, regardless of religious affiliation. This is true pluralism, as opposed to secularist censorship of religion in the public square or government sponsorship of one religion over others.

Secularism, or the avoidance position, would banish religion from any public display on government or public grounds. Secularists do not affirm religious freedom—that is, freedom *for* religion, which was a founding vision in our country's beginnings—but rather they affirm freedom *from* religion. In their understanding, any government tolerance of religion is an illegitimate endorsement. To them separation of church and state means the two are absolutely opposed, and religion should never be allowed to tread on public ground.

Consider, for example, the aptly named Freedom from Religion Foundation, headquartered in liberal Madison, Wisconsin. This group purports to be an educational organization working for the separation of state and church, but its basic purpose is to promote "nontheism"—

anything that is opposed to theism, basically. It identifies itself as an association of "freethinkers: atheists, agnostics, and skeptics of any pedigree," and its church-state views are classic secularism:

> We are not governed by the Declaration of
> Independence. Its purpose was to "dissolve the political
> bands," not to set up a religious nation. Its authority
> was based on the idea that "governments are instituted
> among men, deriving their just powers from the con-
> sent of the governed," which is contrary to the biblical
> concept of rule by divine authority. It deals with laws,
> taxation, representation, war, immigration, and so on,
> never discussing religion at all. The references to
> "Nature's God," "Creator," and "Divine Providence" in
> the Declaration do not endorse Christianity. Thomas
> Jefferson, its author, was a Deist, opposed to orthodox
> Christianity and the supernatural.[1]

This is not a neutral organization, contending for separation of church and state; rather, it is an organization driven by the agenda to debunk historic Christianity and eliminate all references to Christianity or theistic religion in government locales or government-sponsored events. Unchecked, this agenda would lead to undermining or destroying religious freedom in the name of free thinking. In this respect, secularism is truly the enemy of pluralism.

However, distortion at the other end of the spectrum, the acknowledgment position, can be dangerous for religious freedom as well. This view seeks government acknowledgment of religion for, and on behalf of, "the people" at government expense. For example, it would seek government sponsorship of only the majority religion to the exclusion of other faiths. An accommodationist view would seek government's recognition that each student has the right to participate in student-initiated, student-led prayer in public school according to the dictates of individual conscience, protecting the right of both majority and minority groups of students to pray and express their faith in a noncoercive manner.

The acknowledgment position straddles the border of government sponsorship of religion. Paul says nothing in Romans 13 about government taking charge of expounding religion or teaching religion. The last thing we should ever want is for the government to promote religion. That would be like getting hugged by a python: it squeezes all the life out of you, and you fall over dead. Look at the empty cathedrals in Europe. When government sponsors religion, they think they own it, and that's the result. They think they can tell you how to do it, but they never have gotten it right, and they never will.

Roger Williams, founder of Rhode Island and a leading advocate of keeping the government's hands off religion and the spiritual life of its people, had it right in the seventeenth century. His vision for a wall between church and state was not the absolute severance that the

ACLU and Americans United have perverted it to be, but a wall that keeps the wilderness of the world from coming in and corrupting the garden of the church.

That's where the real problem is: not that the church is going to corrupt the world, but that the world will inevitably corrupt the church.

President George W. Bush's goals for faith-based initiatives are noble. I believe there has been a lot of discrimination against religion in American public life, and we can take some needed steps to rectify it. One of the ways that a faith-based initiative can be a powerful tool to help religion become more of a force in American public life is the series of tax initiatives that have been proposed by the president. The most important one would allow nonitemizers to deduct charitable contributions. Seventy million families in this country do not itemize their taxes, and currently they get no tax deduction for their charitable contributions. Under one version of the president's plan, the government's own computers estimate that such deductions would generate $14 billion in new charitable contributions—a sizable portion of which would land in church collection plates. If and when tax reform comes along, we should all support it.

But when the government starts saying, "Let's partner together— you let us use some money to help you provide social services," watch out. Along with the king's shekels will ultimately come the king's shackles. And George W. Bush, a very faith-friendly president, will not always be in office. Imagine if we got into partnership with government during his term and started taking government money to help us provide social services. Then under a later president, the government bureaucrats would say: "Folks, don't you believe in government oversight? If your tax money is going somewhere, you want the government to make sure the money is being spent the way it's supposed to be spent, right?" And now they're auditing your expenditures to pronounce them acceptable or not.

> The salt of the law, when the
> law is on the side of justice
> and righteousness, makes
> a difference.

That's bad enough if the bureaucrats are friendly. But let's say eight to twelve years down the road, a president who is hostile to religion takes office. He or she sends government officials to check your records and make sure the tax money you took was spent only on social services, not for any religious purposes. And of course they will be the judges of what's religious and what's secular. How do you like it then?

Once we start partnering with the government, we compromise our independence. If we let the camel's nose under the tent, before we know it we'll have the whole camel in the tent with us. That's not the road we want to travel.

THE LIMITS OF GOVERNMENT AUTHORITY

Our ultimate allegiance is to God Almighty, not to the government, and if the government requires us to do something that we believe is unconscionable, then we have a moral obligation to engage in civil disobedience—not because we just don't like what the government is requiring, but because we simply cannot do it.

Righteousness in outward forms is never a substitute for personal righteousness.

One of the most important documents of the Civil Rights era was Martin Luther King, Jr.'s "Letter from a Birmingham Jail," addressed to eight white clergymen who, fearing violence, opposed King's civil disobedience. King was jailed on Good Friday, 1963, for unlawful demonstrations against the city's segregationist ordinances. One of the factors propelling his letter to such explosive influence was that he wrote it from a prison in the epicenter of segregation. Dr. King didn't move to New York City and carry on his ministry from there. He didn't move to Los Angeles and call strategic initiatives from there. He personally took his ministry to a town where the injustice was at its worst. The Birmingham Chamber of Commerce bragged about its status as the most segregated city in America. Today Birmingham has an African-American mayor, and it's situated in one of the most integrated parts of the country.

Isn't it wonderful how God changes things? The salt of the law, when the law is on the side of justice and righteousness, makes a difference.

Righteousness in outward forms is never a substitute for personal righteousness. God will not bless us as individuals unless we are personally righteous, and God will not bless us as a nation unless a significant portion of the population is seeking personal righteousness in the power of Christ. But God will also withhold His blessing— God will *judge* us as a nation—if, in our personal righteousness, we are blind to the suffering of others, blind to the exploitation of others, blind to the lack of protection others face because of the unrighteous.

THE SWORD OF EXECUTION

When Paul uses the word *sword* in Romans 13:4 in connection with the responsibility of the governing authorities to punish wrongdoers, it is not the Greek word that was primarily used for the sword of military forces in the Roman Empire. It was the sword of execution, used for decapitation—the preferred method of execution (over crucifixion) for Roman citizens.

The apostle Paul, under the leadership of the Holy Spirit, makes it clear that capital punishment is an option available to the civil magistrate for punishing those who do evil. Notice that Paul is talking about punishment, not rehabilitation. I'm in favor of rehabilitation, but I'm also in favor of punishment. That is a responsibility of the civil magistrate.

Some argue that capital punishment is not a deterrent. I would contend that we don't apply it. Apply it enough, and it's a deterrent. Half of all rapes in this country are committed by repeat offenders. I'd fix that, and cut the rape rate in half by sentencing all convicted rapists who kill their victims to execution, all other rapists would at the very minimum receive life in prison without parole.

If we're going to have a reformation it will always start with a revival among God's people.

Others fear that we might execute an innocent person. There's no record in the last fifty years that an innocent person has been executed in the U.S. True, we have convicted some who were subsequently found innocent before their sentence was carried out, but none were executed. However, several thousand people have been killed by murderers who were let out of prison. That's a lot of deaths of innocent persons.

This doesn't mean that we should ignore injustices related to capital punishment. I think we would all have to acknowledge that in the United States of America, capital punishment has not been equitably and justly applied. If we're going to be committed to capital punishment as a legitimate option available to the civil magistrate for punishing those who have wantonly committed premeditated murder, and I do believe we should, then we need to be just as committed to its equitable and just application.

In the past, you were far more likely to be executed if you were a person of color rather than an Anglo, if you were a man rather than a woman, and certainly much more likely if you were poor rather than wealthy. We have largely eliminated the first two of those prejudices, but there is ample evidence that we have not eliminated the injustice accruing to those who are wealthy enough to hire attorneys who can complicate the death sentence and subvert justice.

Aldridge Ames, a thirty-year CIA veteran, sold U.S. intelligence secrets and identities of clandestine agents, at least nine of whom were executed as a result, to the Soviet Union and Russia from 1985 through 1994. He received a life sentence without possibility of parole. When men like Ames betray their country for money, they are well aware that they are delivering other U.S. citizens and government employees into the hands of death—and not a very pleasant death, in most cases. After

Ames's arrest, the Russians sent a message to him, apparently assuring him that they would keep his money for him, earning interest, until they could find a way to get it to him or his designees. When a reporter questioned Ames about this he said, "Look, there are other people spying for the Russians, and they're looking to see how the Russians treat me."

I'd let the spies see how we treat them. Lethal injection isn't good enough for them. I'd hang them publicly so that other people who want to spy against our country could see what happens if they get caught. I guarantee you, it would cut down on spying.

THE BLESSINGS OF CHRISTIAN INVOLVEMENT IN GOVERNMENT

Government can't bring revival and reformation to America. If we're going to have awakening and reformation it will always start with a revival among God's people. As I said earlier, *revival* is an interesting word: "re-viv-al." You have to get "vived" before you can be revived. Lost people can't be revived; they have to be "vived" first. The first step in revival is God's people getting revived.

Once God's people get revived, they go out and share the Gospel in a new and a more powerful way. Their lives don't compromise what they're saying, and people start getting saved in significant numbers because they can see in the lives of God's people that it works. This leads to spiritual awakening, and as the salt purifies evil and light chases away darkness, awakening leads to reform as the principles of God's Word are applied to the evils of society. Then we have reformation. The contention that awakening and reformation constitute a violation of church and state is a perverted doctrine, twisted and distorted beyond all belief by those who are hostile to religion in an effort to segregate and marginalize us.

Stephen Carter addressed this hostility in his very important book *The Culture of Disbelief.*[2] Carter is perfectly situated to take the governing elites to task without being dismissed as a right-wing bigot. He has the intelligence and wisdom to command attention to his voice. But he also has credentials that enhance rather than diminish his credibility: he's a distinguished professor of constitutional law at Yale Law School (sort of the secular version of the Vatican), he's an African-American, and he's an Episcopalian.

Carter demonstrates that for the last fifty-plus years the various elites in this nation—the cultural, political, educational, and governing elites—have done everything they can to trivialize religion and drive it to the margins of our culture. They have attempted to reduce religion to something you do at home, or something you do at church, with no relevance whatsoever to anything else in human society. To bring religious faith to bear upon public issues, they contend, violates the Constitution. That narrow-minded view is a falsification of what our forefathers intended and an utter distortion of American history.

Let me tell you a little story about John Leland, a man who was saved in Massachusetts during the First Great Awakening in the mid-eighteenth century and became a leading proponent of church-state separation in the cause of freedom for religion. After he became a believer he changed from being a Congregationalist to becoming a Baptist preacher, moving to Virginia and North Carolina, where he was the leading evangelist among Baptists in those states.

Leland's involvement in church-state issues included leadership of the Separate Baptists who were planning to oppose the Constitution because nine of the original thirteen states had tax-supported state churches, and every single one of those tax-supported churches— Episcopalians in the South, Congregationalists in the North, and Presbyterians in middle states—persecuted Baptists.

In fact, in the ten years prior to the American Revolution, the colonial government of Virginia along with its Episcopal authorities jailed over five hundred Baptists for "disturbing the peace" (that's not the worst definition of preaching I've ever heard). The reason for their alleged disturbance? Preaching the Gospel without a license from the Episcopal authorities to do so.

The Baptist preachers said they didn't need a license from some Anglican authority to preach the Gospel; it was their right and obligation to preach the Gospel, and they weren't about to apply for a permit from an Anglican government. And so off they went to jail.

The Baptists planned to oppose the Constitution simply because they were fearful that with a federal government would come a federal, tax-supported, persecuting church. John Leland averted a crisis by cutting a political deal with James Madison: if Leland would get the Baptists to withdraw their opposition and support ratification of the Constitution, under the first Congress of that Constitution Madison would do everything he could to bring an amendment to the Constitution declaring that Congress shall make no law affecting an establishment of religion and there will be no governmental interference with the free exercise of religion—our First Amendment to the Constitution.

In 1791 Leland returned to Massachusetts and resumed his involvement in politics by supporting his friend, Thomas Jefferson, who took office as president in 1801. On Jefferson's first New Year's Day in the White House, January 1, 1802, John Leland arrived as designated head of a delegation to present a gift from citizens of western Massachusetts in appreciation of Jefferson's strong support for religious freedom and his opposition to any imposition of state-sponsored orthodoxy: a cheese wheel weighing over half a ton (that's a lot of cheese, and it was reportedly still being served two years later to less-than-enthusiastic White House guests).

During the ceremony that Friday morning, Leland told Jefferson how he and his colleagues in Massachusetts had been praying for God's blessings on Jefferson, and then he prayed for Jefferson right then and there—can you feature that? A Baptist preacher, praying at the White House. Leland went out of his way to assure Jefferson, "Mr. President, we want you to know that no federalist cows contributed any milk for this cheese; it's a Democrat-only cheese."

Jefferson thanked Leland and the citizens of western Massachusetts for the cheese and went back into the White House. (It is not recorded whether he had any of the cheese for lunch.) That afternoon, Jefferson wrote his famous letter to the Baptists of Danbury, Connecticut, articulating his vision for religious liberty undergirded by the separation of church and state. The Baptists were being discriminated against by the Congregational established state church in Connecticut.

The very next Sunday, less than forty-eight hours later, Jefferson attended a worship service in the House of Representatives, sitting in the front row while John Leland preached a sermon from the speaker's podium, delivered in what was described by one of his critics as a "holy whine" (characteristic of Separate Baptist preaching). Clearly, Thomas Jefferson did not understand separation of church and state to mean elimination of religion from public life, and neither should we. Every major social evil in our history that has been corrected was corrected through the efforts of people of religious faith, who brought their religious convictions into the public arena and said, "This is wrong, and it must be made illegal."

When Abe Lincoln was running for president, he drew a lot of criticism for his vocal opposition to slavery. "You don't understand," they said. "If you keep talking like this about slavery, you're liable to start a war."

Lincoln finally had enough, and one night in Springfield, Massachusetts, he uncoiled his six-foot four-inch frame, stood up straight and looked the audience in the eye, and said that his critics said he should not talk about slavery in politics because that was bringing religion into politics and he should not talk about slavery in the pulpit because that was bringing politics into religion. Lincoln concluded that according to his critics there was no place where he could call this evil thing evil and this wrong thing wrong. I'm glad Lincoln didn't listen to such critics, and neither should we.

Lincoln's critics cited the Supreme Court's 1857 *Dred Scott* decision that slaves weren't people and could still be considered property. This deplorable episode in American history should teach us that the Supreme Court can be, and often is, wrong. It can't tell us what's right and wrong; all it can do is give the opinion of nine lawyers on what's legal and what's illegal—and that's a far different and inferior thing.

These lessons from history underscore that Christians have the obligation to preach the Gospel and lead people to Christ, and all they need from the government is freedom to do that without getting arrested or being coerced by the government's view of religion. We don't want the government sponsoring us to preach religion, or favoring some religion over others. All we need, and all that Baptists have ever needed, is a level playing field. Let the government get out of the way so we can let God's truth loose, and we'll do all right.

However, when people get saved and come to a new understanding, they pass from being children of wrath to children of blessing, from children of darkness to children of light, from children of death to children of life. They have a new perspective, and they have a right to bring that moral perspective to bear on public policy. And if they can convince a majority of their fellow citizens that the reforms are necessary—for example, slavery and racial prejudice are not a matter of consensual behavior between adults in private—they have a right to make certain actions illegal.

That's not a theocracy; it's called the democratic process.

When I was a college student, I used to hear all the time in Baptist churches and conservative circles that "you can't legislate morality." Nonsense. What they really meant at the time was they didn't want any laws against segregation. Today it's the liberals who are saying you can't legislate morality. What they really mean is they don't want any restrictions on a woman's alleged right to kill her unborn baby anytime until he or she is fully delivered from their mother's body.

Laws against murder, laws against theft, laws against rape, laws against racism—these are all legislation of morality. When we pass such laws, we are not so much imposing our morality on murderers and thieves and rapists and racists as trying to prevent them from imposing their immorality on their victims. Because in all these incidents somebody is doing harm to somebody else against their will, and we have an obligation to make it illegal and put the civil magistrate on the side of right and those being victimized, not on the side of evil and the victimizers. When government is on the side of evil, it perverts the reason God established government in the first place.

Now if we want America to be a Christian nation, there is only one way to do it, convert it through evangelism and discipleship. It can't be done by law. It can't be done by artificial legislative fiat. To turn America into a more Christian nation we have to help people get saved, and then to help them understand that being saved means they're going to have a different value system and need to live out those values in and through Christ in all three divinely-ordained institutions: family, church, and government.

Our ultimate allegiance does not belong to any political group or any candidate or the party that mom and dad voted for or the party that dominates the community in which we live. Our ultimate allegiance belongs only to Jesus Christ, and we ought to vote our values, our beliefs, and our convictions as informed by Holy Scripture and let that take us where it will. If you don't like your voting choices, get involved. I don't care which party you get involved in. I deal with both major parties every day of the week and, trust me, right now both of them can use more help than all the Christians in America can give them.

Wouldn't it be wonderful if we could live to see the day when abortion is no longer a partisan issue, when both parties were absolutely committed to every human life being welcomed and affirmed and the only disagreement was on the best way to implement that commitment? That's how far we've come on race. Nobody in America except extremist fringe groups want to go back to the way it was. Both parties are committed to racial reconciliation. The only difference of opinion is over the best and most effective policy strategies to achieve the desired ends.

That should be our goal, to remove killing babies in the womb as a partisan issue in America. But it won't happen until God's people get right with God, and God's people begin to be the salt and the light that God called us to be, and God's people understand that the Bible is true not just in our homes, and it's true not just in our churches, but it's true twenty-four hours a day, seven days a week, and therefore we are called to look at everything through the worldview of God's Holy Word and seek to bring every institution in society under the sway of the Gospel of Jesus Christ.

That is our obligation: to make the civil magistrate more and more reflect the values of the people, to make certain that the people are getting converted and that those who aren't are at least operating from a values perspective compatible with biblical teaching. But one of the reasons we're in trouble is that we have allowed the world to tell us that we don't have the right to be involved in public policy.

You have just as much right as every other citizen to be involved in public policy, and you have an obligation and a commission from your Lord and Savior. You are to be the salt of the earth and the light of the world.

I pray that God will help us to understand that rearing our children in the nurture and admonition of the Lord is the responsibility of the family and the church, not the government, but that we do have obligations and responsibilities in relation to the state. I pray that God will call some of our young people He has created and knitted together in their mother's wombs to come forth and be godly public servants. Public service is a calling, and I pray that we will all be open to whatever calling God desires for each of our lives. God has created each of us for a purpose—for some that is full-time public service; for others, full-time Christian service in ministry, for others, full-time family service. May each of us be open to God's leadership in our lives, to long for becoming the instrument God would have us be, to bring about the revival, the awakening, the reformation that our nation so desperately needs.

13

THE DIVINE TIPPING POINT

In the America God will bless . . .

- Internet pornography purveyors will be going broke for lack of business.
- adult bookstores will be closing their doors for lack of customers.
- liquor stores will be cutting back on inventory.
- bar owners will be cutting back on their hours.
- popular culture will be far less brutal, coarse, vulgar, obscene, and sex-and-violence obsessed.
- ambulances will not be rushing to the sites of drunk-driving accidents.
- divorce courts will be on quarter time.
- husbands will not be leaving their wives, and wives will not be leaving their husbands.
- more men will be fulfilling their responsibilities as husbands and fathers.
- fewer children will be born out of wedlock.

- children from conception onward will be cherished as gifts.
- many more children will be raised in the admonition and nurture of the Lord.
- all children, in Christian homes or not, will be valued and mostly safe from abuse.
- there will be less need for foster care and more volunteers to be foster parents, with more parents willing to adopt.
- there will be fewer single-parent families, and therefore reduced economic and emotional stress on women.
- fathers will be more present in families, resulting in many fewer mothers with children aged six and under living below the poverty line; in fewer juvenile males in the criminal justice system; in fewer girls involved in early-onset of sexual activity; and in significantly reduced promiscuity.
- public schools will have better across-the-board performance and fewer discipline problems among students.
- the spread of sexually transmitted diseases will be drastically curtailed.
- giving to churches and charity organizations will be significantly increased.
- society will be more caring and compassionate to its own members and to its neighbors.
- the elderly and infirm will be honored instead of neglected and warehoused, with greater family involvement in their care.

- there will be no need for, or incidence of, assisted suicides.
- life at both ends of the human cycle will be reverenced rather than threatened.
- abuse of women will be the exception rather than the rule.
- there will be sharply reduced sexual and racial discrimination.
- Americans will be more likely to consider everyone equal in the sight of God.
- we will be more compassionate toward sinners and the needy because we will recognize that "there but for the grace of God go I."
- we will not presume upon, or think that we deserve, favor on our lives because we will know that God alone is the source of blessing.
- there will be more citizen politicians than career politicians, and interludes of public service will be routine for most people.
- most if not all of the population qualified to vote will be registered, with equal numbers participating in all stages of the political process.
- political campaigns will be less negative and more focused on legitimate issues.
- more people will seek the best interests of the country rather than of their interest group.
- government will more closely reflect the people, and a more righteous people will produce a more righteous government with godly leadership.

- there will be a lot of unemployed dope dealers.
- pressures on the penal system will be eased because fewer people will be in prison.
- retribution will be balanced with rehabilitation, and sentences for heinous crimes will be carried out swiftly.
- feeding the hungry and housing the homeless will have a higher priority with lower levels of government involvement because the churches will be taking responsibility to do it.
- Christians will be proactive in providing safety nets for widows, orphans, and those in need of help.
- there will be more believers, less disconnect between belief and behavior in those who profess to be Christians, and more positive views of Christians among unbelievers.
- there will be a significant increase in numbers of churches and in numbers of those attending regularly.
- God will raise up generations of godly men to be the spiritual leaders of our churches.

INFECTING CULTURE WITH THE GOSPEL

Best-selling author James Michener wrote a novel that departed from his sweeping, geographically based sagas, drawing mixed reviews from Michener fans but enthusiastic praise from writing and publishing circles. This is most likely because *The Novel*, a mystery centering on a struggling writer near the end of his career, is an inside look at writing and publishing from four different points of view: writer, editor, critic, and reader.

The editor is a loyal champion who has shepherded her writer across several books, and she is fighting to keep her publishing house, on the verge of a corporate takeover, from dropping him as a has-been. She believes in his talent and keeps hoping that he will hit it big with the next book, because he has been building a readership over the years and the situation, she thinks, is ripe for a breakout title—a book that will catapult him to successful renown.

Malcolm Gladwell might say that the editor is anticipating that moment when the author's readership builds to a critical mass and the next book proves to be the change agent that explodes his sales by an exponential factor—the "tipping point" in his career, spreading his fan base like a virus racing through a population to epidemic levels.

Indeed, the virus metaphor is exactly what Gladwell uses in his book *The Tipping Point: How Little Things Can Make a Big Difference*[1] to describe how major changes in our society often happen suddenly and unexpectedly. Ideas and behavior, Gladwell believes, can be infectious, creating social epidemics:

> A tipping point is that moment in an epidemic
> when it reaches a critical mass; it's the point on the
> curve when the epidemic starts to take off. The AIDS
> epidemic tipped in a matter of months in the early
> 1980s. The flu tips each year—there's a week every

winter when everybody suddenly has it. One of the characteristics of epidemics is that there's this moment when they take off. I think that's a very useful metaphor to describe some social phenomena.[2]

The three central elements of a social epidemic, Gladwell says, are (1) those who transmit the infectious agent; (2) the infectious agent itself; and (3) the environment in which the infectious agent is operating. An epidemic will spread more quickly or more slowly depending upon the quality and effectiveness of each of these three agents.

For example, in the first element—those who do the transmitting—only certain kinds of people can transmit effectively. Gladwell calls this The Law of the Few:

> [Epidemics] are created and sustained by very small groups of exceptional people. It is important to identify just who the socially influential types are in any audience that you are trying to reach. In some ways, that is a harder task than the standard advertising model which assumes that all customers are of equal importance.[3]

In the second element, the infectious agent, the variable is the relative strength and quality of the agent, or infection. This is The Stickiness Factor. Paul Revere, for example, had a very sticky infectious agent in his message of alarm, "The British are coming!"

And the third element, the environment in which the infection spreads, can be weak or strong in its reaction to the infectious agent. Gladwell identifies this variable as The Power of Context. The colonists reacted immediately to Revere's message, uniting to meet the advancing British solders with determined resistance.

Let's plug in Gladwell's model to our 2 Chronicles 7:14 vision for the America God will bless. (1) Christians are the transmitting agent. Living out the Gospel of Jesus Christ in obedience to God's Word and empowered by the Holy Spirit, they are prime small groups of exceptional people whose influence is created by the power of God working through them.

(2) The Gospel of Jesus Christ is the infectious agent we carry out into our culture. In this book, I hope to transmit the infectious agent of God's promise in 2 Chronicles 7:14 to the hearts of Christians who will be seized with a vision for the America God will bless, beginning in their own hearts.

(3) For revival among Christians, the environment is the church, the "my people" of God's promise. Will we respond with a great longing for healing and renewal? Will we devote ourselves to the conditions God sets forth—humbling, praying, seeking God's face, and turning from our wicked ways?

As we seek to be salt and light in the world, we carry the infectious agent of the Gospel to the environment of our desperately needy, fallen world. Will we transmit the Gospel effectively, in word and deed? Will we seek the conversion of hearts even as we seek to bring all areas of life, including the social order, under the sway of Jesus Christ?

We know that the Gospel has an absolute magnitude of the "stickiness factor" in receptive hearts. We can commit ourselves confidently to obedience in the Lord, compelled by the love of Christ, knowing that as Christ's ambassadors we have been entrusted with the ministry of transmittal; that we are spreading nothing less than the truth of the Gospel—God's ministry of reconciliation through Christ. The power of context rests with the power of the Holy Spirit in receptive hearts, so we know that we do not minister in vain.

We don't know what "critical mass" is according to God's definition, and we don't know when the moment might arrive when He will say "*Now,*" spreading an epidemic of Christian ministry and influence across America. Therefore we can release all anxiety about when that glorious tipping point might occur, laboring obediently in simple trust that God's promise will one day be fulfilled, releasing the power of His blessings upon our country.

But we do know that each of us can start here and now. The real hard spade work will get done privately. Corporately, we can all pray for it—and we do need to pray for God's blessing, for revival and spiritual awakening. We can pray, "God, revive us again." Make us into the men and women, the husbands and the wives, the mothers and fathers, the singles, the families, the church members, you want us to be. We can encourage and exhort one another to become the people God wants us to be, but this change will happen one heart at a time.

> *As* we seek to be salt and light in the world, we carry the infectious agent of the Gospel to the environment of our desperately needy, fallen world.

Certainly we must not forsake the assembling of ourselves together—in worship, in the ministry of the Word, in Bible studies, in prayer groups. None of us can become all that God wants us to be separately and alone. Only together can we grow toward the fullness and stature of Christ. But the inward transformation will take place privately, as each of us allows God to move in our hearts. I can pray for you, and you can pray for me, and that is a good and beneficial thing. But only *I* can let God do what He wants to do in my life. And only *you* can let God do what He wants to do in your life.

If God is going to bless America, it will begin with Christians getting right with God. That's the starting point.

"In the spirit of Christ, Christians should oppose racism; every form of greed, selfishness, and vice; and all forms of sexual immorality, including adultery, homosexuality, and pornography. We should work to provide for the orphans, the needy, the abused, the aged, the helpless, and the sick. We should speak on behalf of the unborn and contend for the sanctity of all human life from conception to natural death. Every Christian should seek to bring industry, government, and society as a whole under the sway of the principles of righteousness, truth, and brotherly love."[4]

The Future of Our Country

Whether America has a future worth having doesn't depend on what happens in Washington, D.C., it doesn't depend on what happens in the Supreme Court or in the Congress. It depends on what happens with you, and people just like you; and your family, and families just like yours; and your church, and churches just like yours, with godly pastors after God's heart; and political leaders at all levels of government across America.

My prayerful hope is that when they write the history of the first decade of the twenty-first century they will go to an old folks' home somewhere—and by the way, if we win this struggle for America's souls, there'll be old folks' homes; if we don't, don't count on it, because the same arguments that are used to abort unborn babies can be used to euthanize old people. They'll go to an old folks' home somewhere, and they'll find some harmonic-convergence new-age guru who smoked too much dope and inhaled it, and they'll stick a camera in front of him and ask, "What happened to you, man? It looked like you had all those fundamentalists, evangelicals, Baptists, and traditional-values folks on the run—and then all of a sudden it just blew up in your face."

Only I can let God do what He wants to do in my life.

And he'll shake what's left of his ponytail, and he'll say, "Yeah, it's a bummer man, it's a bummer." Then God will grant him a rare moment of lucidity, and he'll say, "Yeah, man, you know it's like that guy we read about back in high school, you know—uh, uh, that Admiral Yamamoto dude. He was the genius who planned the Japanese attack on Pearl Harbor. When the first reports came in of the stupendous success of the attack and the devastation of the Pacific Fleet, they were celebrating on his flagship in Tokyo Bay.

"But then further word came that they hadn't broken off negotiations and then attacked as originally planned—(instead, they had commenced the attack while they were still negotiating in Washington). Yamamoto canceled the celebration, went into seclusion in his stateroom and wrote these words regarding this teaching in his diary: 'I can think of nothing which will infuriate the

Americans more. At Pearl Harbor we had hoped to strike a crippling and a demoralizing blow, but I am fearful that all we have succeeded in doing is to awaken a sleeping giant and fill him with a terrible resolve.'

> *Whether America has a future worth having depends on what happens with you and people just like you.* ◠

"That's what happened, man! Those religious people got all fired up and started comin' back at us, and what happened next just blew our minds, because it wasn't what we were expecting . . . no, it wasn't. . . ."

I believe if you look out across the landscape of America today with the eye of faith and you listen with the ear of hope, you will recognize the stirrings, and you can hear the rustlings of a long-slumbering giant called the people of God as they are awakened from their spiritual slumber. Like the prodigal son, they shake the filth from themselves and rise up and determine to go home to the Father, who scans the horizon waiting for that which was lost to come home. And they are determined that as they go home to their heavenly Father they are going to take their country with them.

Obedience is a wonderful thing. We know that our problems are beyond our reach, but we also know that allowing God to do a marvelous work in our lives is not beyond our reach. Obedience opens up our lives and allows God to change us, to accomplish His purposes through us. It's totally within our control to repent of our disobedience, to pray and seek the Father, to depend on God to hear and respond. If we are going to be about our Father's business, we will want God to be shaping us into the people He wants us to be. We will be seeking to help others discover the joy of repentance and return, so they can become all that God wants them to be.

> If God is going to bless America, it will begin with Christians getting right with God.

If enough of us do that, then God is going to bless America, more richly than we can imagine. That's the tipping point.

May it begin here. May it begin now. May it begin with you, and may it begin with me. God, please bless America. *Amen.*

ENDNOTES

CHAPTER 2, A PROMISE FOR OUR NATION?

1. "Half of All Adults Say Their Faith Helped Them Personally Handle the 9-11 Aftermath," September 3, 2002, Barna Research Online, www.barna.org.

2. Excerpted from Article XV, "The Christian and the Social Order," of *The Baptist Faith and Message,* adopted by the Southern Baptist Convention, 14 June 2000.

3. John MacArthur, *Can God Bless America?* (Nashville: W Publishing Group, 2002), 86.

4. Ibid., 78.

5. Ibid., 72–74.

CHAPTER 4, HUMILITY, AMERICAN STYLE

1. Douglas MacArthur, in a speech before Congress on April 19, 1951, text available in multiple public records.

2. John F. Kennedy, in a speech at American University on June 10, 1963, text available in multiple public records.

CHAPTER 5, SEEKING GOD IN PRAYER

1. Billy Graham, *Just As I Am* (San Francisco: Harper Collins, March, 1999).

2. Alfred Lord Tennyson, from his poem "The Higher Pantheism" (public domain).

CHAPTER 6, TURNING THE TIDE OF *WHOSE* WICKED WAYS?

1. Bob Woodward, Bush at War (New York: Simon & Schuster, 2002), 259.

CHAPTER 7, WHEN GOD HEARS AND RESPONDS

1. See Proverbs 3:34, James 4:6, and 1 Peter 5:5.

2. Quoted by Michael Ciccese in "Lantz Restores Faith in Truckers, Faith in Prayer," American Trucking Association, www.truckline.com, 6 November 2002.

CHAPTER 9, THE FAMILY GOD WILL BLESS

1. *Hardwired to Connect: The Scientific Case for Authoritative Communities: A Report to the Nation from the Commission on Children at Risk* (New York: Institute of American Values, 2003), 15.

2. *Why Marriage Matters: Twenty-One Conclusions from the Social Sciences* (New York: Institute for American Values, 2002).

CHAPTER 10, THE CHURCH GOD WILL BLESS

1. I am deeply indebted to my longtime best friend, Dr. Paige Patterson, President of Southwestern Baptist Theological Seminary in Ft. Worth, Texas, for essential insights into the 13th chapter of Hebrews and their application to the church God blesses.

2. Richard Baxter, *The Reformed Pastor,* ed. Rev. William Brown, M.D. (London: The Religious Tract Society, n.d.), 112–13.

3. Thomas Oden, *Agenda for Theology: Recovering Christian Roots* (San Francisco: HarperCollins, 1979), 11.

CHAPTER 11, THE COMMUNITY GOD WILL BLESS

1. John MacArthur, *Can God Bless America?,* 87.
2. Ibid., 74.

CHAPTER 12, THE GOVERNMENT GOD WILL BLESS

1. From the Web site www.ffrf.org, maintained by Dan Barker, spokesman for the organization and self-proclaimed "Minister Turned Atheist," who moved from "fundamentalism to freethought" after nineteen years in evangelical ministry and has since devoted his energies to decrying everything he used to believe.

2. Stephen L. Carter, *The Culture of Disbelief: How American Law and Politics Trivialize Religious Devotion* (New York: Basic Books, 1993 / Anchor paperback, 1994).

CHAPTER 13, THE DIVINE TIPPING POINT

1. Malcolm Gladwell, *The Tipping Point* (New York: Little, Brown, 2000; paperback Back Bay Books, 2002).

2. Malcolm Gladwell, from an interview in *The Atlantic Unbound,* March 29, 2000 (The Atlantic Online, www.theatlantic.com).

3. Malcolm Gladwell, from an interview on the book chat page of CNN online (www.cnn.com).

4. *The Baptist Faith and Message,* Article XV. "The Christian and the Social Order," adopted by the Southern Baptist Convention, June 14, 2000.

NAME AND TOPIC INDEX

Scripture Index